SHELTER FROM

A Life Affirming & Inspirational Journey

TREVOR E. PRICE

SRA Books
Sue Richardson Associates
Minerva Mill Innovation Centre
Station Road
Alcester
Warwickshire B49 5ET
T: 01789 761345
www.suerichardson.co.uk

Mr. Tambourine Man
Written by Bob Dylan
Copyright ©1964; renewed 1992 Special Rider Music. All rights reserved.
International copyright secured. Reprinted by permission.

A CIP record for this book is available from the British Library.

ISBN 978-0-9567553-0-8

Designed, produced and published by Sue Richardson Associates

Printed and bound in Great Britain by TJ International, Padstow, Cornwall

Contents

~ Dedication ~

For my beautiful, darling Chris who made my life so complete that I never realised just how whole I was until you were taken away…
…every day for more than 42 years you gave me 'Shelter From The Storm'.

You showed us all what courage really means.

'As a teenager Chris was bright-eyed, full of fun, usually unimpressed by authority and unfailingly generous of spirit. How wonderful it was that she never changed.' *Val & Peter Halman*

'I'm going to miss my sweet friend Chris. She always knew that the important things in life were mostly simple things - family, friends, a good laugh and lots of sunshine.' *Deb Hanfeld*

This book is also dedicated to our adored grandchildren Oliver and Harriet Price, who lost their beloved tickle monster Granny too young but are my inspiration to continue living…

Any profits from this book will go to the two charities Pancreatic Cancer UK and Pancreatic Cancer Action. If you wish to make any additional donations, please find their contact details below. Please let them know that your donation is in Christine's memory. Thanks.

Pancreatic Cancer UK
www.pancreaticcancer.org.uk
020 3177 1686.

Pancreatic Cancer Action
www.pancreaticcanceraction.org
05600 685917

Introduction

Chris and I in August 2008 at the wedding of Becky Jackson and Kris Thompson in Cyprus. Just four months later Chris was diagnosed – unbelievable!

~ Introduction ~

On 9th January 2009 my wife of 41 years, Chris, collapsed. When Chris was subsequently diagnosed with inoperable pancreatic cancer two weeks later, we were, as you would expect, both devastated. Over that weekend our son Robert and his family – wife Pippa, children Oliver (then 10) and Harriet (then 6) – came up from Bath to be with us. It was a strangely surreal time.

But by the time the weekend had finished it had become apparent to me and to Chris that we were going to need more than just Robert's support. We took the decision that there would be no hiding away; that we would face Chris's battle together and in full view of the world. We would ask all our family and friends to help us fight the battle in whatever way they could.

On the evening of Monday 26th January 2009 I sent an email to about 200 friends, family and business acquaintances telling them Chris had been given a very short time to live. Little did Chris and I know how our basic plea for help – inherent in the email – would lead to a level of support that would sustain us during the next 348 days, inspire in us a fight against the pancreatic cancer and sustain Chris so that she 'lived a miracle'.

This is our story of 2009, based upon my monthly update emails and our supporters' emails, letters and cards in response. It is given as a tribute and thank you to them all – our wonderful family, friends and acquaintances. It is based completely upon those communications, the words that gave us our inner strength. It was this support that gave both Chris and I 'Shelter from the Storm'.

It is written in the hope that if we can help just one terminally ill cancer patient (and their loved ones) to open their heart to the world and ask for help, then it will be worth it for the support that they will receive. If you are in this situation please, don't hide away. Let people help. It will make the battle easier and so much more fulfilling.

The book is written with a grieving heart, still raw from losing my beautiful Chris far too young. But written also with a sense of pride in her fight, in awe at her courage and with humbleness at the goodness of our family, friends, acquaintances and even strangers who helped us in our hour of darkness.

Thanks Chris, for all our wonderful times together over those 42 years.

God bless you always. I love you and I miss you more every single moment than anyone can ever understand.

Bewdley, England - August, 2010

Starting Over

~ John Lennon ~

The Look of Love, February 2009

~ Starting Over ~

Friday 23rd January 2009, 4.30 pm.
I arrive home from my Utility Warehouse leadership training.
I've had a good day, plenty of good learning and it resurrected
my enthusiasm. Chris is outside the front door, wearing her
coat, either putting something in the bin or sorting out the
ashes from the fire.

As I cross the patio, I shout out, 'Are you cold? Still
wearing your coat?'

Chris walks back into the house, saying 'I've only just come
in. I've been down the doctor's'. I follow her inside.

The world as I know it is about to be changed for ever.

I say 'Your results are back?'

'It's cancerous', and Chris subsides into my arms, tears
streaming down her face. I cry. We cry. We hold each other.

'What did he say?'

'Cancer of the pancreas. It's inoperable.'

We sit around the kitchen table. We cry. We hold each other.
We try to understand what has happened to us.

I phone our doctor. His secretary returns the call, saying he
will visit us at home after surgery. Chris has a coffee.

I fire up the computer and type in the dreaded words – cancer
pancreas.

I look at the screen through my tears. I feel empty. As
I read the information my worst fears are realised – there
seems to be so little time. Two to four months seems to
be the average survival expectation. I can't bear it. I picture
the funeral. I picture our grandchildren. I cannot comprehend
anything. Simply shock.

I print off pages from websites. I drink tea. We hold each other again. I love my Chris so much, I cannot imagine a life without her. Utter desolation surrounds me.

6.20 pm
Dr Simon Gates arrives at our house. We receive the explanation. Inoperable. Prepare for the worst. Chemotherapy. Spread outside pancreas. Come and see me again on Monday. Liquid morphine. I can't bear it. I can't believe it. Chris is unbelievable. Calm & collected. Such strength. I love her so much.

7.30 pm
I telephone Robert, our only son. I break down on the phone. We're both crying down the line. He wants to come up but I say no, come tomorrow, bring Oliver & Harriet to see their Granny. It is unbearable that Chris won't see them grow up.

9.30 pm
I go to the pub as normal. We've agreed I should go and break the news to our pals. We both can't stand the thought of people pussyfooting around the subject. We want them to be there for us, and they all love Chris very much. I hate going out on my own, always have.
I perch on a bar stool, buy a pint. Stare into the distance. Brenda Haines comes up, asks how Chris is and I say 'She's got cancer'.

It's like being a ghost in a dream.

On Saturday morning, after a restless night, I went to buy the papers as usual. I didn't come straight home but called at Chris's great friend Ann Baker to tell her the news. Ann had lost her husband to a brain tumour in February 2007. It was a tearful cup of tea we drank.

Later that day I suggested Chris go across the lane to tell her best friend Sandra Jackson. 'No, you go and tell her.' So, over I went. More tears. More disbelief.

Robert, together with Pippa and our two grandchildren Oliver and Harriet came up on the Sunday. Inevitably there were tears when they came in. Chris was probably the most calm of all of us, perhaps already showing the pragmatism and courage that we would see over the next twelve months.

Pippa came prepared with a list of questions that we should ask the doctor. I think she had spoken with all of their medical friends! Neither of them seemed to have accepted the hard facts in the way Chris and I had – that she had limited time and that there was no magic cure. Robert was his usual logical self but I could see there was fear in his eyes. He was to have trouble coming to terms with this over the next few weeks.

I remember the day as almost normal – sort of 'There's this issue, but maybe we've got it wrong in our understanding'. As always, the focus was on Ollie and Harriet but Chris was not well. She was in pain (her only medication was paracetamol at this point) but she was hiding the truth, refusing to let the world see the real pain. Just the second day of 351 days of courage.

Over the weekend Sandra found out the name of a liver/pancreas cancer expert at Queen Elizabeth Hospital, Birmingham. Already the benefits of asking for help were appearing, even though I think Sandra herself was bordering on being an emotional wreck.

I spent almost all weekend on the internet attempting to gather information. I had virtually no sleep at all. Three to four months' survival was written about a lot, which was a scarily short time frame, but that appeared to be our scenario. Chris wasn't very impressed with this news, immediately deciding (to herself at this point) that one year was her minimum as she targeted her 60th birthday in December. I later learned she had told Robert that she 'wanted to be around for Christmas'.

We saw our GP again on Monday 26th January having taken the weekend to try to absorb the news. I'm not sure if I ever really did absorb it.

The appointment gave us nothing new and no better hope. He would provide the documentation to enter the benefits system, but it was documentation that gave Chris less than six months to live. That bit of paper was a very cold dose of reality to me.

We needed to enter the benefits system, after all I had retired from the moment Chris gave me the news. There was no discussion or external thoughts on this decision. Chris and I never needed to discuss it, it was the easiest of all decisions.

Robert summed this up to Ollie and Harriet in his usual brilliant way. 'Granny has looked after Grandad for over 40 years, now it's Grandad's turn to look after her'. Simple, you see!

26th January 2009

Hi All,
I am sorry to send a rather impersonal email but it is the quickest way to inform you of some heartbreaking news.

I'm sorry to tell you that Chris has been diagnosed this weekend with cancer of the pancreas. The cancer is inoperable. We are awaiting consultations with a pancreas specialist at QE Hospital in Birmingham and an oncologist here in Kidderminster, who will explain the options available, which include chemotherapy and radiotherapy.

Cancer of the pancreas is particularly vicious as it is almost always only found when it is far too late for surgery, as with Chris. It is also aggressive in its timeframe – the average survival time after diagnosis is two to four months, although there are cases of over two years and it is upon these we are basing our hopes although tempered with the realism of the average.

Chris really is not well, with quite severe pain always present. She is taking 24-hour painkiller treatment. Our plans to sell the house have been abandoned, and sadly our hopes of returning to travelling to see all our friends in UK and around the world will be unable to take place. Chris already finds travelling small distances uncomfortable. Foreign travel is impossible.

I will let you know the outcome of the consultations in the next couple of weeks but ask for your prayers. Until we have those consultations it is impossible for us to plan what the next months of our life are going to be but if you would like to visit us we would be delighted to see you.

All our love,
Trev & Chris xxx

Hi Trev,
Utterly devastated to read your e-mail – really can't believe it. I am so, so, sorry.

Puts everything into perspective – there's us fretting over a too imminent move to Cornwall.

I'm in a state of total shock over your news – will call shortly but be assured of our prayers and best wishes.

Your friend,
Ken (Lewis)

Ken had been a friend since his days as a very important decision maker within the company that was my biggest customer when I was in corporate life. We go back over ten years. We had spent time with him (and his wife Tammy) in 2008 when Tammy and Chris had gone off, together with their local pub landlord, flying in his private plane while Ken and I flogged our way around yet another golf course together.

Dear Trevor,
I read your e-mail just now. I am really sorry to hear your news.

You and Chris will be in my thoughts and prayers at this very difficult time. Please let me know as and when you have further news. In the meantime I will be thinking of you both and praying that you do hear something more positive.

With love and best wishes,
Andrew (Hartley)

Andrew was a long-standing friend from my life in BASF, where he was the company lawyer. Andrew and I share a mutual love of Manchester United, having attended several games at Old Trafford together.

Hello,
I just read this ... we are both so sorry to hear this terrible news.

We WILL pray for you, Chris, we have found that it has worked for us in recent tough times – I really mean that!

Steve Jobs (founder of Apple Computer) has survived pancreatic cancer for a few years now, and Patrick Swayze seems to be holding his own - so it is not impossible to believe that there is hope.

I will write again - be optimistic!
Love to you both from Geoff and Susan (Owens)

Geoff is my longest standing friend. We attended primary school in Worcestershire together back in 1952! We also attended the same senior school in later years (good old Kings of Worcester). Over the years we have visited him so many times in California I've lost count. We know all his family, and he has always been a solid rock in our lives. A wonderful human being who has given deep friendship to us both over the years.

Whenever I'm in trouble I ring Geoff in the middle of the night - often now on Skype - where he provides a level of support that is awesome. I think Chris and I both knew Geoff (and Susan) would be important over the forthcoming months. We were correct.

My dear Chris,

My love, my thoughts and my prayers are with you. I wish I could wrap my arms around you and Trev and take away this terrible pain. I hope that the power of all the love from your family and all your friends around the world will give you some strength and comfort as you fight this terrible thing.

Mountains of love and oceans of prayer and well wishes are with you 24 hours a day,
Deb (Hanfeld)

Deb was one of Chris's closest friends (and had been since 1988). Married to Horst, my boss and business mentor, over the years the two of them became ever closer. Chris virtually became Deb's assistant nanny in London after her first son Andy was born.

Deb introduced us to her whole family in Australia and we counted them as very special people in our lives. Chris visited Deb two or three times (last time in 2005) on her own after Horst died suddenly and tragically in 1998. They shared a sense of humour that was very dangerous! I knew that Deb would be important for Chris, and so it proved. She visited England, and was in text contact every day with Chris throughout the year. She was an inspiration to Chris, and those texts were really important in keeping Chris going over the year.

Dear Trev and Chris,

To say I was shocked and upset is fatuous. I opened your mail thinking it was about John Jordan and I am writing this with a sad and heavy heart. I have not yet said anything to Florence as I know it will choke her up and it is late.

We have recently lost a dear friend with this horrible disease and it is the most diabolical of all the cancers. He could not cope with therapy as he had a chest condition and advances are constant so we can never lose hope. Trevor it is so very difficult for you to cope with this and I cannot comprehend your private hell.

Chris has always been such a resilient lass and to even contemplate her losing her dignity is not easy but survival is the priority.

I hope you understand this is coming from the head and the heart although it is just as the thoughts are entering my head at the moment. You are one of the sincerest and you always wear your heart on your sleeve so this must be incredibly rough for you in a series of rotten breaks.

Our thoughts and prayers are with you both,
John and Florence (Oliver)

John and Florence became our friends in Sheffield in 1970. John was my supervisor when I worked for Cadbury Cakes. During those two years in Sheffield they helped us two young kids grow up, all be it with a somewhat unusual approach to adulthood. Loyal, glorious Geordies, John and Flo remained in our hearts even though we didn't see them very often. That didn't matter, they were solid, real friends not ships passing in the night. We felt their love shining through their notes to us.

Trevor, Chris,
So sad to hear your news ... We want you to know our thoughts are with you both and the family.

Trevor ... Don't hesitate to contact me if you need any assistance with anything.
Lou x x (Cresswell)

I met Louise back in 2005 when I started my new business networking business. Lovely lady, her husband Neil is rapidly becoming a veteran in Afghanistan - brave, hard work.

Dear Trevor,
I am so sorry to hear your news about Chris. What do any of us do to deserve such things? If you will excuse the use of the word, Chris is lucky to have her inner strength supported by you and the family at such a difficult time and I know that you will handle this as well as is humanly possible.

Yes, Chris will be in our prayers and I hope she can buck the trends and averages and continue to share her life with you.

Best regards,
Tony (Mills)

I've known Tony since back in 1989 when we were tutors together at the Leadership Trust. Tony (and his wife, Chris) have encountered their own deep tragedy with the loss of their young daughter Isobel some years ago. Our friendship overcomes long gaps in our meeting together, proving that friendship has little to do with regular contact. It was a real comfort to know that they were praying for us to beat the averages.

Hi Trevor,

I am so sorry to hear your news. I will keep my fingers crossed about the time frame too.

I just wanted to let you know that my thoughts are with you both.

All the best,
Helen (Dowling)

Helen is a business contact made in the last four years. She is the proof that at times of trouble, if you ask for support, it will be forthcoming.

Hi Trevor and Chris,

Judy and I are so very sorry to hear your news and we wish you all the very best. You will be in our thoughts and prayers.

We really hope you have encouraging news from the consultants.

Please keep us informed of progress and please let us know if we can be of any help or assistance. If we can get up your way soon we will arrange to pop in to see you.

All our love,
Rob & Judy (Price)

Cousin Rob has always been a reliable part of the Price family. It was good to know that the whole family were 'on board' with us. Rob lost his mother to cancer when she was virtually the same age as Chris. History repeating itself is not good news.

Chris, Trevor with all our love and prayers. I know there is nothing we can do but if you need anything shout.

Julian and Netty x x x x x (Turner)

Julian and Netty are friends from Bewdley who we didn't see that often, but who we felt we could always rely on. We were correct.

Hi guys,

Shocking news. I only hope that the prognosis is as good as it can be.

I don't get down to Bewdley much these days. Since we lost my mum, my dad tends to come up to see us in North Notts, rather than the other way around. However, I will try to call by when I'm next in the area.

Love to both of you. Stay positive.

Adam (Archer)

We've known Adam 30 years, which in itself terrifies me. He used to play in the pub pool team with Robert and me all those years ago. He lost his Mum to cancer a couple of years ago, so this whole thing probably reawakened bad memories.

Trevor,

I was very sorry to learn of your sad news. Luck certainly hasn't been an ally in recent times. I'm not certain what to say that would be of any comfort other than to convey my deepest sympathy and wish that hopefully fate and a little measure of good fortune will allow you both to spend more precious time together.

Sincerest best wishes,

Paul (Johnston)

I worked with Paul for twenty years or more. He sadly lost his wife desperately young and has brought up his children alone – something of which he should be very proud. It was great to hear from him, to know there was someone else I could talk to who had experienced the loss of their lady.

Hi Trevor,

I am really sorry to hear the news.

However it is not too late to turn this around. I had a friend three years ago who was diagnosed with an incurable inoperable brain tumour. It was too big to operate on and the doctors were very negative about his future prospects. Like pancreatic cancer a brain tumour is usually an irrecoverable situation. His head was swollen up, he could not see and was in agony and his family were convinced he had a couple of months at best.

Three years later the tumour has reduced significantly and is almost gone, through a combination of radiotherapy and natural/complementary methods that assisted what the doctors were doing. If nothing else the complementary methods that are available will significantly reduce the pain and suffering.

What my friend experienced is known as spontaneous remission. It is well documented and happens to thousands of people in the UK every year. The link below will give you a little bit of information:

http://majidali.com/remissio.htm

If you want me to come round and share the options with you then let me know. I could come over and see you on Friday evening or on Saturday during the day if that is of any help. I will not be offended at all if you feel that this is not appropriate for you or Chris.

My thoughts are with you both,
Damien (Deighan)

Damien became a friend through my business networking. A genuinely kind man, Chris decided not take up his alternative treatment advice. His concern touched us both.

Hi Trevor and Chris,
We were both so sorry to hear this awful news and of course you will be in our thoughts and prayers. Please stay in touch and we wish you both the best for the future. Sometimes life seems so unfair, doesn't it? We pray that you will receive inner peace from ours and others' prayers.

Love,
Dave & Di (Morgan)

Cousin Diane is the oldest daughter of my wonderful Auntie Mary and Uncle Jack (my Mum's brother). They are such a lovely family, whose priorities in life completely reflected mine and Chris's. It was so good to know they would be supporting us.

Dear Trevor,
What dreadful news to come into this morning, I can't believe it, poor Chris... I know she's a brave girl and a fighter and with your love and support you'll both do everything possible... It goes without saying that you'll both be in our prayers every night as well as Robert and the family... Do keep us in the loop.

Our love to you all,
John & Claudia (Hutson)

I worked with John 30 years ago and we have stayed pals ever since. We have enjoyed dinners out many times, where Chris and Claudia would chat away about the children whilst John and I put the business world to rights! John put us in touch with some alternative healing options but Chris decided that she would prefer to stick with conventional medicine.

Dear Chris and Trevor,
What devastating news! We are truly shocked and dismayed. Our thoughts are with you as you make your way through this terrible time. We hope that the specialists

can give you some pain-free, good-quality time, Chris, to enjoy with your family and friends as well as some hope and comfort in the time ahead. You've always been a fighter; don't give up. We feel quite useless at this distance, but we're sure you are enveloped by much love and support. Even from afar, we would love to add ours.

We are distracting ourselves with the happy memories of the wonderful time we spent with you last year and hope that you will soon get some positive options from the medical consultants.

Much love for now,
Laurie and Linda (Vogler)

Laurie is Debbie Hanfeld's brother. Over the years, they have become close and important friends to us. As part of their European tour in 2008 they made time in their schedule to attend our 40th Anniversary Party. Whenever Chris was over in Australia, some time was always spent in Brisbane with them. During the year we received regular phone calls from them checking how Chris was and sending their love. They actually spoke to Chris the day before she went into hospital in December.

Please let us know when visits are done and we can come over.

All our love and prayers,
Philip and Val (Burton)

We know Phil and Val from our golf trips to Spain. Val & Chris used to joke about all the time during the week!

Trevor & Chris,
I'm so sorry to hear your news, send Chris my love. Please do keep in touch with the outcome, my thoughts are with the both of you and your family.

I have spoken to Paul, he's on the road today he hasn't yet seen your email. I'm sure he will be in touch either by phone or email later on today.

Perhaps when Chris feels up for it we can visit soon. I know she feels uncomfortable travelling but if you both fancy some sea air at anytime you are both welcome to stay.

I will get Paul to arrange a visit to yours soon.

Love
Sue X X (Blake)

Sue is the wife of my friend Paul, who worked with me in my Emtec days.

Trevor,
We're so sorry to here this news. Marilyn and I will remember you both in our prayers. Please let us know how Chris progresses.

God bless you both.
David & Marilyn (Dippie)

I worked with Dave for twenty years at BASF, where we became good friends. Their constant prayers and support throughout the year really helped keep us positive throughout the year.

Dear Chris and Trevor,
We are devastated to hear your news, and very sorry that the current prognosis is so bad. Please both be assured you are definitely in our thoughts and prayers and will keep vigilance that you will still be able to follow your dreams and travel in the very near future.

Chris, many of these situations are only overcome by strength of mind and faith that anything can and does happen.

All our love and prayers,
Paul, Monica and Charlotte (Silver)

Paul and Monica live in Chile these days. Paul was a business acquaintance in recent years, and he and Monica came to our 40th anniversary party. Their support and prayers meant that actions really were being generated around the world.

Hi Trevor,
Very very sad to hear your bad news Trevor – as if life hasn't been cruel enough to you guys already. It's something we all dread I guess and there certainly doesn't seem to be any reason or logic to it does there? But fight all the way – Hilary was told she had a particularly virulent strain but wouldn't accept it and kept going for four years.

Our thoughts are with you and love to Chris.
Richard and Jan (Price)

Richard is another cousin whose sister Hilary fought a long battle with breast cancer in the not too distant past.

Dear Trevor,
We were devastated to read the news about Chris's illness, we still find it hard to

believe. We can't begin to know how you two are feeling, all we can do is to send our love and pray that dearest Chris finds the strength to beat the odds.

If you feel that we might be able to help by visiting, writing or in any other way, you only have to ask. You are in our thoughts.

With love,
Val and Peter (Halman)

We've known Peter and Val for 45 years! Peter was one of our bosses when we worked (and met) all those years ago at Cadbury Cakes in Worcester. We've stayed in touch over the years, meeting regularly at the Cadbury reunions Peter organised, and also at long weekends in Bude, Cornwall when a few ex-Cakes people met up. Peter and I compete every year for The MinRoll Challenge Cup - a virtual cup played on the golf courses of Badgemore Park and Wharton Park. Their friendship over the years has been enduring and precious to us, while Peter's awesome wit has kept us entertained on many an email.

Hello Trevor,
Both Carol and I are completely shocked with your very sad news. There are no words to convey how absolutely sorry we are to hear about Chris and her condition.

I am currently outside of the UK – but will contact you when I get back later this week, to see if we can arrange a suitable day/ time to meet up. Our prayers and thoughts are with you both.

Love,
Gary & Carol (Milner)

I employed Gary as a national account manager at BASF. He worked for me, and with me, over a ten year period. Chris and I have been delighted as his career has developed and progressed. Carol is a teacher, and we have spent happy weekends with them talking and laughing as we sorted the world's problems out!

Bad news indeed, with God's help Trevor you and the family will give each other the support to get through the coming months.

Love,
Mick & Pat (Hewitt)

Mick was a colleague at Cadbury Cakes in Sheffield way back in about 1970/1. We've stayed in touch over all the intervening years, meeting at the Cadbury Cakes reunions along the way.

Trevor,

Many thanks for this. I have sent it on and it will find its way to many of my friends in the Church and elsewhere. My thoughts and prayers are with you and Chris.

Regards,
Robert (Geary)

Robert was my commercial solicitor from 1997 onwards and has become a personal friend over the years.

Trevor & Chris,

We are really sad to hear the news. It is very difficult to know what to say and to say nothing is not the right thing either. Obviously you will both be very much in our thoughts and let's hope that the consultants can give you both something a little positive.

Please do let us know how things go and we both send Chris our very sincere wishes and love.

Regards
Sharon & Tim (Woolridge)

Tim and Sharon are neighbours with whom we shared a love of all things musical - especially Bruce Springsteen!

P-----pray

U----until

S----something

H----happens

If you'll do this for me... I'll do it for you...

When there is nothing left but God, that is when you find out that God is all you need. Take 60 seconds and give this a shot! All you do is simply say the following small prayer for the person who sent you this.

Father, God bless all my friends and loved ones in whatever it is that you know they may be needing this day! And may their life be full of your peace, prosperity and power as he/she seeks to have a closer relationship with you. Amen.

Then send it on to five other people. Within hours you caused a multitude of people to pray for other people. Then sit back and watch the power of God work in your life.

When Jesus died on the cross, he was thinking of you! If you are one of the 7% who will stand up for him, forward this with the title 7%. 93% of people won't forward this.

Hi to you both,
I received a call from Sue this morning to relay the heartbreaking news in your email sent last night. I was two and a half hours into a four hour car journey to one of our company factories. To say I was absolutely stunned must be a huge understatement, particularly compared to the feelings that you two must be engaging with right now. All I could do was pull over and try to comprehend this news.

Thoughts of your Christmas letter and the sheer determination you two have and the utmost belief in your own abilities as a couple to overcome adversity were all I could comprehend. You both have coped with so much already and had drawn a line in the sand on the issues and frustrations in order to move forward, even preparing yourselves to sell your beloved home in order to travel and keep in touch with all your friends. What I did deduce from my time spent reflecting on your situation was that you are both of equal strength but together you have a combined energy, determination and belief that is without doubt unequalled.

If anybody can join together and repel this evil it is you two. After everything you have battled against over the years and the mounting stress that situations (and certain people) have cruelly enforced on you, this must be the one battle that, although the biggest, your combined belief can conquer.

One of your recent emails reflecting on the S & A scenario also came to mind as it demonstrated an incredible resolve that you have (at least outwardly) bottled up and tried to deal with, with the utmost professionalism. But it is exactly that kind of calmness when faced with adversity that Chris will need from you to help her through these tough times.

So my time in the lay-by didn't help me to understand the hows and the whys, or even what would be the right things to convey to you in your troubled times. But what it did say to me loud and clear was that you two have the most powerful resolve and deepest love for each other that somehow through everything to come that you will both be able to fight this together and in the many months to come with the help of all your friends, blossom once again.

Sue and I will of course come up and pop in for a coffee and catch up with you both, we will let you know when we are free over the next few weeks. No doubt you will have a lot of friends calling in and as Sue said if you both want to get away from it all for a few days when Chris is up to travelling (either by car or train), we are only a couple of hours away, which may be doable? A bit of sea air down on the South Devon coast might be a welcome break for you both. As you know my 'race' diary is pretty full this spring so equally if you want to spend some time down here on your own you are both very welcome to stay anytime when we are away also. You only have to ask.

Take care and god bless, I will email some dates when we can pop in to see you.
Sue and Paul x (Blake)

Paul worked for me at Emtec and over the years we became good friends. When he married Sue, Chris and I visited them down in Devon. They are a lovely, warm couple and we had some good times with them. Paul is an epic marathon/half marathon runner!

P-----pray
U----until
S----something
H----happens

Been doing this since I first heard! Not really sure what a sinner like me can achieve!

Thinking of you both.
Tony (Loynes)

Tony is Chris's youngest brother. Over the year I think he sometimes struggled to come to terms with her illness. We didn't see much of him, but he kept in touch by phone on a regular basis, calls that cheered Chris up when she received them.

Trevor,
Our thought and prayers are with you at what must be a very difficult time for you and your family.

Love and best wishes,
Chris, Claire & Georgina (Hallett)

Chris was a friend I met through business. We had a go at getting a new business up and running (together with Louise Cresswell) but it never really took off.

Dear Trevor,

We were really shocked by the news about Chris – just shocked.

It's only a couple of weeks since we were reading your Christmas letter, and felt like a corner was being turned – that you had a new plan, with more travel, more everything. This is a cruel blow, and we feel it, too.

There's nothing I can think to say – we just want you to know we are thinking of you both, and hoping for the best. And we especially ask that you pass onto Chris our cheers of encouragement, for every bit of fight and every bit of determination – we're in her corner, too.

If will power is enough, then collectively, we have the will power.

Our very best wishes are with you both. Thinking positive thoughts.

Best regards,
Tim (MacLachlan)

Tim and Vicky are more friends from Australia! Tim and I met at conferences when we both worked for BASF (and then Emtec). We were drawn together by speaking English when most of the conferences were held in German. Chris and I stayed at their beautiful home on Mornington Peninsula outside Melbourne, and we have met them on their visits to Europe. They have two great sons, and when we first visited them Tim arranged a tour of Melbourne for us all by speedboat. Spectacular!

Hello Trevor,

I am very, very sorry to hear this news. I will remember you in my prayers.

God bless,
Lyn (Taylor)

I helped Lyn in a mentoring capacity when she set up her own business.

Hi both,

We cannot tell you how saddened we were to hear your awfully sad news, what a horrible shock for you all. We will pray for you all at this very worrying time.

Lots of love,
Jan & Dave (Norton)

Jan and Dave looked after us for a good few years when they were the landlords of The

HopPole in Bewdley. We had some seriously funny moments with them at the pub – great days that always brought a smile to our faces because of all the stories. It was good to hear from them as we hadn't seen them for quite a while.

Dear Trevor,

Ken has passed on your email regarding Chris. I am so sorry. This sad news must be more than heartbreaking for Chris and you and it is dreadful that Chris clearly is in a lot of pain. For you I guess, you must feel so bad that you cannot alleviate the pain. However, knowing how caring you are I am sure you are doing everything humanly possible for Chris. All I can say is you will be very much in our prayers and thoughts.

Best regards,

Keith (Fleming)

Keith was a business contact from my BASF / Emtec days, a high-flying senior manager with a variety of major retailers. We don't see Keith that often but it was so good to know that he was supporting us through our dark days.

Hi Trevor,

So hard to find the right words, thinking of you both. I would like to meet but would have to come by train. Will try and contact you tomorrow.

David (Gilbody)

I worked with David in the late 70s/early 80s at BASF. We've stayed in touch over the intervening years. Our paths had crossed occasionally, and I know David has had some tough times with his marketing business. It is a tribute to his durability and his skills that his business survives today, but probably it is because of his unfailing optimism! During 2009 David proved to be a wonderful friend, someone who telephoned every couple of weeks to see how Chris was doing but primarily to make sure that I was surviving it ok.

Hi Trev,

Just read your e-mail and my heart has sunk, after reading such a positive one from you only a few weeks back it just doesn't seem fair that life has kicked you right back down again. I know how much you must be trying to hold things together but I also know that your heart must be breaking. Just believe that if all your family and friends could pray together and wish Chris a speedy recovery she would be better tomorrow because you have an awful lot of love and respect from us all. I'm thinking of you both and you know that if there is anything that I can do for you then you only have to ask.

Lots of love,
Chrisy x (Cross)

Chrisy was my personal assistant at Emtec. A lovely lady who is now a policewoman. It was great to hear from her.

Dear Trevor,
I am absolutely devastated to receive your email. I really am so very sorry to hear of this news and I wish both you and Chris the very best of good fortune in this situation. If there is anything at all that I can do to help on the business front, then you really must let me know. Sometimes it is just a helping pair of hands here and there that can make all the difference so do please call on me if you think I could help you.

In the meantime I will be thinking of you both.
Tim (Kidson)

Tim is a recent business acquaintance who shares a love of Bob Dylan and Manchester United with me.

Trevor,
I have been working at Excel London this week and have only just opened your email. Chris, yourself and all of your family must all be devastated by this sad news. Both mine and Tina's thoughts and prayers are with you both.

Our love,
Jeff & Tina (Hull)

We've known Jeff and Tina for over 35 years, in fact since we moved to Bewdley. We participated in school pantomimes when our children were at primary school, and we've stayed in touch over the years.

Dear Chris & Trevor,
We have just picked up your email and are absolutely shattered at your very sad news. We hope the outcome of the consultations gives you more positive news and you have years rather than months together. Our thoughts and prayers will be with you both and your family.

Love,
Pat and Brian (Bourne)

Brian and Pat were customers in Birmingham when I was a sales rep at the beginning of my

BASF career. Over the years we've had the occasional meal together and their support was unflinching during the last year.

Dear Trevor and Chris,

I was more than sorry to hear your bad news. I know a little about cancer of the pancreas. My younger brother died of it. He was diabetic and did not look after himself, so that his illness was almost self-inflicted.

There is so much they can do these days, so don't give up hope yet. Chris seemed to be so well a few months ago. Your Christmas e-mail sounded so full of hope and plans for the future. So, again, one never knows what is in store for us. In Germany, one is supposed to have yearly check-ups on these type of organs as pancreas, liver, kidney, etc. and blood tests. Whether a problem would be immediately discovered, I don't know. The most common cancer these days seems to be connected with bowels, but pancreas is more seldom, I think.

Anyway, it sounds that Chris is in good hands with a specialist.I will go to Church again on Sundays and pray for Chris. I will naturally include her in my prayers!

With my best wishes to you both,
Love, Ulla (Pschierer)

Ulla was my secretary at BASF (and to all the previous Divisional Directors before me!), so we have known her over 30 years. She now lives in Germany, and it was so nice to receive her support across the European frontiers.

Dear Trevor,

Really bad news. I feel with you and Chris and of course we will pray for you and for Chris every day and it is our hope that our good is able to help if our hope is gone.

Best regards and our best wishes to both of you,
Ulrich (Volz)

Ulrich was Logistics Director at BASF/Emtec. We kept in touch at Christmas time, so it was good to receive his support.

Dear Chris & Trevor,

We have been so stunned by your very sad news concerning Chris that words to form a reply have been very difficult to find. We have tried to imagine how you both must be feeling. The sense of injustice and the disappointment at the situation, the hurt for yourselves and that which is caused to your loved ones.

The plans that can't be fulfilled. It is at these times that we turn to a power much greater than our own and ask for His help. We believe in God and know that if you ask for His help he will give it. He will help you to remember all the good times in your life and how you struggled to overcome the hard and testing times and how you succeeded. Here is another testing time but together and with His help we know you will cope.

We pray for you and your family.

Our love to you both.
Anne & Alan x x (Pitt)

We've known Ann and Alan since we first moved to Bewdley. We've shared many a laugh at events with them, and as with so many friends their prayers were so important to us.

This is the Optimists' Creed. It will help you get better.

Thinking of you and yours,
Edward (van der Kleijn)

Promise Yourself

To be so strong that nothing can disturb your peace of mind.

To talk health, happiness, and prosperity to every person you meet.

To make all your friends feel that there is something worthwhile in them.

To look at the sunny side of everything and make your optimism come true.

To think only of the best, to work only for the best and to expect only the best.

To be just as enthusiastic about the success of others as you are about your own.

To forget the mistakes of the past and press on to the greater achievements of the future.

To wear a cheerful expression at all times and give a smile to every living creature you meet.

To give so much time to improving yourself that you have no time to criticize others.

To be too large for worry, too noble for anger, too strong for fear, and too happy to permit the presence of trouble.

To think well of yourself and to proclaim this fact to the world, not in loud words, but in great deeds.

To live in the faith that the whole world is on your side, so long as you are true to the best that is in you.

Edward is a recent business friend, who is one of the most positive human beings it has been my pleasure to know. The sending of 'The Optimists Creed' gave Chris and I some inspiration in facing up to the challenge ahead.

Trevor,
I am so sorry to hear your terrible news.

If there is any thing that me or Fiona can do please let me know.

If you want to use our house for a base for a trip into London you are very welcome.

We will be thinking of you,
Paul and Fiona (Bradford)

Paul was my finance director at Emtec. He's a kind and supportive person, also a rare example of an accountant with a commercial mind! We had a splendid weekend with Paul in Brussels some years ago.

Dear Trevor and Chris,
Our love and prayers are with you.
Cousin Clare & Paul (Farrands)

Clare is my cousin. Her elder sister Hilary passed away from breast cancer a few years ago.

Christine.
Thinking of you more than words can say!

Loads of love sent to you.
Alex & Seany Leigh (Tomlinson)

Alex is my sister Rosemary's eldest grand-daughter, Seany Leigh her first great grand-daughter!

Dear Chris.
We are so sorry to hear of your illness - our hopes and prayers go with you.

With all our love,
Judy, Reg & family(Parmenter)

Reg and Judy are long standing friends here in Bewdley. We have spent many hours laughing at Reg's wonderful sense of humour, often at his son Dale's renowned parties. Reg and Judy are an inspiration to us because together they have overcome some serious health issues themselves but kept cheerful in the face of those adversities.

Dear Christine.

I was so sorry to hear about your illness.

No doubt, you ask 'Why me?' I know that with Trevor's care and your family's support, you will not give up hope. After all, you had to be brave and optimistic once before, if I remember rightly! Perhaps some of our prayers will be heard. I wish you all the very best, that you cope with the pain you must be in but don't give up!

With love,
Ulla (Pschierer)

To Chris.

We are so sorry you have this problem. Never give up, all we can cross is crossed for you.

Loads of best wishes.
Ron & Pat (Perrins)

Ron is one of our drinking buddies at the local pub. Chris has known Ron and Pat for years, ever since she worked at the Old Town Hall Stores. Ron's sense of humour, with his range of ridiculous but hysterical jokes, kept me smiling when I was having some dark days during Chris's illness.

Chris & Trevor,

Just a quick note to let you know we are thinking of you at this difficult time. All our prayers are with you.

Lots of love,
Heather, Mark, Sammi, Craig, Alex & Seany xxx (Tomlinson)

Heather is my niece, youngest daughter of sister Rosemary.

Aunty Christine,

Know that you are in our thoughts at this worrying time, that you are in our prayers in your time of need and that your wellbeing is close to our hearts always.

With much love from all of us,
Lesley, Dean, James & Lewis xxxx (Carpenter)

Lesley is also my niece, middle daughter of my sister Rosemary. Lesley always referred to 'Aunty Christine'. This use of 'Aunty' always has a hugely emotional effect on me because it reminds me strongly that it is not only me that has lost someone very special but others as well.

~

Robert drove up from Bath to be with us when we saw the liver specialist, Dr Isaac, in Birmingham.

The Liver Unit didn't take private patients but we obtained a referral from our GP and sent copies of the scans. We saw Dr Isaac on Friday 30th, when he confirmed the diagnosis. Inoperable. A small 'spot' in the liver. He told us the team at Wolverhampton/Kidderminster were excellent.

We were still in shock. In these circumstances it is difficult to recognise yourself that you are suffering shock. You actually think you are ok, but when you look back the reality is utterly different. You go through the motions of life, but your head simply isn't in its normal place. Chris was ill – we knew that – and we were trying to control her pain with paracetamol and liquid morphine. In truth, this was all rather ineffective and within a couple of weeks we had a successful project in place using slow-release morphine.

Our first meeting with our oncologist consultant, Dr Mehra, was on February 6th, with treatment to start on February 19th. There was no great transfer of information, simply confirmation of diagnosis. He told us to arrange a meeting with nursing staff in the Millbrook Suite at Kidderminster Hospital who would explain the details of chemotherapy treatment and the potential side-effects.

Chris never considered not having the standard chemotherapy treatment. We investigated dietary treatment potential, researched other alternative treatments (at this time I was barely sleeping as I spent all night on the internet trying to find a magic cure) but she was never convinced that this was the route for her.

The reality was to emerge that the support of our family and friends from around the world would be more successful than any alternatives. This doesn't mean we rejected their strengths. It was simply that Chris herself (and it can only be the patient's decision) was not prepared to refuse the standard treatment(s) in the hope that alternatives would work. Sadly, with the exception of the Penny Brohne Centre, it seemed that with all the alternatives you had to refuse chemotherapy/radiotherapy to be able to participate.

We had our meeting in the Millbrook Suite. We were told all about Gemcitabine, the drug that would be used. It was explained that Chris would be having treatment on a regular cycle – once a week for three weeks, then one week off. She would have to take a blood test every week to check that she was well enough to receive the chemotherapy.

The possible side-effects were explained as well, which all made pretty unpleasant reading.

I still didn't really believe this was happening. I knew it was true but didn't actually accept it. I thought the experts were wrong. I thought we could 'make it go away'. This sort of stuff didn't happen to people like us. We had always overcome all our difficulties, we would overcome this. Die? Nonsense! The treatment would make Chris better, like when she nearly died before in 1988 with her aneurism.

Chris with our son Robert - they had a wonderful relationship together
(February 2009)

FIELDS OF GRAY

~ Bruce Hornsby ~

~ Fields of Gray ~

As you have seen, the response to our initial email was overwhelming. There were also so many letters and cards that I don't have room to include in this book. The level of support that was forthcoming was truly amazing. It inspired Chris from that day forwards throughout her illness. Being alone to fight cancer was, in our opinion, the worst option.

You need inspiration. Anything that gives additional reasons to survive and fight is good. It is too easy to sink into despair, feel sorry for yourselves and begin to believe that you are the first people this has ever happened to, which of course is nonsense.

We are blessed with so many friends. They were all so crucial to Chris battling on and being so positive. They gave her reasons to believe. When I read those emails we received, they almost always reduce me to tears. They flooded into the mailbox and began the support process that became so important to us. It was not a difficult decision to send out the email telling everybody of Chris's illness. It seemed the natural thing to do. We were in trouble – the biggest trouble anyone can ever face – and being alone to face it simply wasn't our style.

All our life together, Chris and I had friends to whom we could turn; to ask for help when we needed it. This was not only emotional support, although we needed that sometimes in our 42 years together, but also practical help. After all, I am the worst DIY bloke in the world! So when it came to informing all our friends of our forthcoming battle it all seemed very natural.

What the response to our situation shows is that human beings almost always want to help. As we read these instant responses Chris and I knew that we had too many people on our side not to fight the battle. As the months went on, this constant stream of support meant that we never became depressed but were always being uplifted, on an almost daily basis, by the mails, letters, cards and actions.

Our friends in Ireland, Tony and Ann Killoran, immediately travelled to a religious community in the West of Ireland (Poor Clare Monastery of Perpetual Adoration, Drumshanbo, Co Leitrim) where the nuns dedicate every waking day praying for the sick. Chris was added to their list, and she received by mail the trappings from the monastery. They never left her side in the whole year.

Candles were being lit every week for Chris across the world – America, France, Germany, Australia, Ireland, England, Scotland. Positive thoughts were transmitted across the oceans and mountains. Love came pouring out to us from all sides. Distance healing was started. Not all these actions are reflected in the email base of this book. If I had tried to add the phone calls (in particular) and letters to the emails, this book would be double in size! It was truly incredible.

With every message we received, hope was stirred and our fight strengthened. I have absolutely no doubt that 'living the miracle' was directly the result of these supportive actions being linked to Chris's over-whelming survival spirit. When you added all this to her determination to enjoy her last months with us and be with us as long as possible, you can begin to understand how we were able to take such a positive attitude.

I would like to offer fellow cancer sufferers some advice. Don't retreat into yourselves and try to deal with this monster alone. Open your hearts to your friends, be upfront with your illness. Often people want to help but don't know how to. They may be embarrassed. They have absolutely no idea what to say. 'Sorry' seems utterly inadequate, so they say nothing, maybe even not contacting you when they do hear about your cancer.

These are the people who struggle to deal with it at all. They were probably terrified that Chris would suddenly turn into a wasting, weight losing person, screaming in painful agony or drugged to the eyeballs and being miserable. That she might be blaming the world and being bitter. I suspect that may be a pre-conceived idea of death by cancer. The reality was that Chris was more inspirational in her last year than she had ever been before her life. Our friends who couldn't deal with her cancer were, in reality, the biggest losers of all because they missed this amazing woman proving that cancer and forthcoming death could be dealt with in a fearless manner.

This is a waste of the great human ability to support one another. You can read the emails and letters we received. That's why I've written this book.

As a thank you to our friends, a tribute to them for having the courage to say to us 'We cannot imagine what you are going through but we are going to help you deal with it.' People were magnificent. They became part of our battle. They wanted to help once they knew and understood that we needed them to help.

Their involvement meant that Chris knew she was not alone. But also that, as I retired to become her full-time carer, I also had support upon which to draw. Do not underestimate how important this was to us both. It meant I had people to call when I was low, as well as Chris receiving encouragement every day of her year-long battle.

These early days were very, very difficult. We were trying to establish the correct level of pain relief. This takes weeks, rather than days. It is an incredibly frustrating process because the patient suffers along the way. We eventually moved to slow-release morphine. The initial dose was (in our view) high but by trial and error we soon had it reduced to 10mg in the morning and 20mg at night. Chris stayed at this level for almost the whole year. It is the greatest example of how our living miracle developed – that her pain control was always this low, resulting in her always being 'with it' and thus being able to maintain her high quality of life, the most important thing to both of us.

Chris was back in hospital on Sunday 1st February, constantly vomiting, unable to eat or drink and getting weaker by the hour. The weekend GP cover was crap, and hospital was the only option as it appeared I knew more than the attending doctor

Chris was only in hospital for one afternoon and night. They fuelled up her liquids, restored her equilibrium and gave us some advice on the painkilling regime. We were in the experimentation stage because neither of us felt that big doses of liquid morphine, linked to the daily dosage of slow release morphine capsules, were the answer. Throughout the year we only used liquid morphine as a last resort - never as part of Chris's daily pain control routine.

January 30th	Consultant: Pancreas Specialist (Dr Isaac), Queen Elizabeth Hospital, Birmingham
February 1st	Hospital – The Worcestershire Royal Infirmary
February 6th	Consultant: Oncologist (Dr Mehra), Millbrook Suite, Kidderminster Hospital
February 10th	Chemotherapy Information, Millbrook Suite, Kidderminster Hospital

9th February 2009 – Update No 2

Hi

I thought you may like an update on Chris's situation now that we have had two consultations with specialists. Firstly though, I must thank everyone for all the wonderful messages, kind thoughts, prayers, telephone calls, cards, email messages and unbelievable support you have shown us over the last three weeks since this bombshell took over our lives. They have been so important to us both as we have struggled to accept the position and are proving a source of inspiration to us. There are prayers being spoken all over the world, together with positive thinking and a deep belief that together we can help Chris to overcome the cancer. We have to believe miracles can happen!

We have now seen a pancreas specialist at Queen Elizabeth Hospital, Birmingham and an oncologist at our local cancer unit at Kidderminster Hospital. Both have confirmed, in their opinion, the tumour is inoperable and Chris has decided she will be treated with chemotherapy initially. At the same time we are using some alternative healing and researching to see whether there are any clinical trials taking place from which she could benefit.

Both consultants have given a survival timeline of 9 months – 1 year, but gave examples of survival longer than that. It is to these that we cling. Whilst this is an utterly awful timeline, bearing in mind that the original timeline suggested was much shorter, this information actually managed to create a feeling of relief and success – which was a very strange emotion indeed!

Chris in herself is amazing. She is constantly tired, unable to walk far without getting exhausted and in constant pain that is being treated with a cocktail of painkillers which includes liquid morphine. Through all this she never complains, and despite having been rushed into hospital last Sunday, has had a pretty good week since they sorted her out on that visit! Her sense of humour remains intact, and now that we know her treatment programme begins on 19th we are starting to make our plans for holidays and visiting our lovely friends. We need to plan visits in with her treatment, and we refuse to consider that she may not be well enough to participate – we are staying positive and know that with our family and friends' help life will continue to be on the good side!

Thank you once again for your support and prayers, hopefully we will be able to meet before too long.

All our love,
Trev & Chris
xxx

Hello Trev & Chris,

Trev, I got your phone message (eventually – I didn't realize it was there until Sunday) and I could not hear all that you were saying because you were speaking softly and the transmission was distorted. However I think you were saying basically what you just wrote here.

Well you have to take this as good news. I don't know exactly what you talked to Julian about – but I don't know anyone who has a better handle on faith issues. He is a man of considerable faith and it always seems to work for him no matter what the situation and he has been a great help to me in recent times. If you need to talk to someone about this – just call him – he will be happy to hear from you.

We are all praying for you Chris. Be brave and ask God for healing through Jesus Christ. It does happen. Ask Julian, he has experienced it personally.

We'll talk...
Love Geoff (Owens)

Hi Trevor,

A mixture of good and sad news, but thank you for this, it must be very difficult for you to document in this manner. Both Tina's and my thoughts and prayers are with Chris and yourself.

Unfortunately we have a very similar situation at this present time with the wife of my oldest friend. I have known Martin since I was 4 years old, last year Martin and Emma, his wife celebrated their ruby wedding. In July 2008 two brain tumours were discovered and operated on separately, then it was found that Emma has lung cancer, the aggressive strain. Like Chris and yourself their lives have been turned upside down.

Take care and of course our love to Chris.
Jeff & Tina x x xx (Hull)

Thanks for the update.

It is of course rotten and unimaginable to hear this awful prognosis. You are both approaching it with such fortitude, it is very humbling. We just say again you are always in our thoughts and prayers. Every day brings advances.

Take the greatest care,
John and Florence (Oliver)

Hi Trev,

We really appreciate you giving us an update on Chris. It sounds harrowing, but we take heart that Chris retains her sense of humour, despite all. It's impossible for us to imagine what you're both going through, but we're doing what we can in terms of positive thoughts and crossed fingers. So, again, please pass on our very best wishes.

It's been a dreadful week here in Melbourne too, with some terrible stories emerging from the bushfires. Thankfully we have not been directly affected at all – the nearest fires were a few kilometers away, and the worst of them about an hour's drive from here. But you'd never know it, as the wind has taken the smoke away from Melbourne.

With your situation and the bushfires here, it's been a timely reminder of how lucky we are, and how tenuous luck can be. I reckon it's about time luck turned for you guys, so hang in there…

All the best,
Tim (MacLachlan)

Thanks for the update on Chris. Sorry we didn't make it on Sunday. The weather in Muskoka was very bad. I am in St Albans at the moment but back tonight. I actually have a delivery in Mamble tomorrow to do! We will either pop up tonight or tomorrow.

Is that ok?

Much love to Chris.

Love you mate xxxx
DG (David Grandison)

Dave and Marie are long-standing friends, virtually family. Unbelievable support all year!

I have been sending healing thoughts to Chris along with my mum and great aunt, we are all spiritual healers. It won't cure but you never know may help in some little way.

Mandy xx (Cottle)

Mandy looks after our back-office for my work with NRG. It was lovely to know even more distance healing was taking place.

Everyone try praying this:

God, grant me the grace to accept with serenity,
The things I cannot change,
Courage to change the things which I can change
And the wisdom to know the difference.

And it is ok to stumble into a church, most of which are usually kept open during the day, and get on your knees and just talk to God as a friend and 'father'. God is not a foreboding entity to be feared, only respected, and He wishes to be understood and will use this to bring you closer to Him.

I often feel like praying to God: 'Please give me a better job/ more money/stop this horrible thing from happening'. But the best results came, for me, on being able to accept that nothing happens for no reason, and that although the world appears to be in chaos, it is clear from the Bible alone, that everything is pre-ordained. Your friends need a lot of empathy - which you have, having lost your father. Give freely! Me and John have faced so many 'Goliaths' in the photographic industry - so many things going against us, but we still stand where others have fallen. Why? I pray that God will give me enough to survive. Not the Porsche, but enough. I have enough!

Love,
Jen xx (friend of David Grandison)

Hi Trevor and Christine,
We have just read your e mail and we are so so sorry to hear your bad news. What can anyone say when this terrible c word appears in your life.

I will pray for you both and wish we were still near so we could lend our support. You are both wonderful people and have the love of your family and friends all around you. If there is anything Dickie and myself can do let us know we will pray for you and your family and keep Chris in our thoughts. God bless you both.

Love and thoughts,
Chrissy and Dickie (Probert)

Dickie and Chrissy were the former landlords at our local, The Runnning Horse. They were fantastic hosts and are greatly missed by us regulars.

Hello Trevor and Chris,
Hope you are both ok and we hope Chris's treatment is going well. Are you still in

turmoil and trying to come to terms with this awful blow to you both? We hope and pray you get the strength from somewhere.

Regards to you both,
Tony and Ann (Killoran)

Jim and I were horrified and saddened to hear that Chris has this cruel and devastating inoperable cancer. We send you both our fond loving thoughts - it is wonderful how courageous people such as Chris and sadly other of our friends can be – some inner strength seems to help and support at this time.

With love from us both.
Jim and Joyce Williams

Jim was one of my original colleagues when I joined BASF in 1976! Still in touch after all these years.

Something

~ The Beatles ~

On Tresco, Chris in her pink woolly hat!

~ Something ~

We began February with a photographic session. Our good friend Kim Sharman gave us this sound advice – take some nice photographs of Chris before she starts chemotherapy. It was a smashing Sunday and Rob organised the photographer. He and Pip came up with Ollie and Harriet. We had a make-up lady come to pamper Chris before the session. She looked so beautiful that day, and the photos are a lovely remembrance of her.

This is a really good idea for anybody who finds themselves in our position. Don't hesitate, do it. These photos will become very important to you over time.

It is at this point that I am going to deliver a bit of a financial lecture. Now, all who know me will find this rather amusing, as I can waste money for England! If spending became an Olympic sport, then I would be England's best hope for a gold medal.

Chris is the opposite. She is a natural manager of money, understands value better than most and never wastes money. She is also far sighted (or maybe she had a premonition). In 2007 she told me that we should have life assurance on her. At that point we only had some on me in order to cover the mortgage. We couldn't really afford it either but we had no serious savings available for such a crisis due to the business failure in 2005/6.

'Nah', said I, 'If anything happens to you I'll go back to work.' Naivety is a terrible thing!

Chris insisted. So, we took out 50% of our mortgage value on her. Term insurance is relatively cheap insurance. I plead with you all to consider this as well – preferably for both of you. Why? Because Chris's policy contained an early release clause that if survival diagnosis is less than 6 months, the company pays out in advance. It was truly our life saver, the enabler for us to enjoy our remaining time together.

Because, let me tell you honestly, fighting cancer, being positive, taking trips and holidays, organising photo sessions – these are expensive. It is a lot easier if you have resources. The thought of fighting this battle without what were effectively unlimited resources fills me with horror. I am not sure what the effect would have been on us both. So if this little book does one thing, I hope it inspires you to take action. If ever you get struck by cancer in your family like we were, you will be more than grateful to the life insurance company!

Lecture over!

What Chris's early, strong treatments achieved was to destroy the speck of cancer that was in her liver. Her first three chemotherapy treatments completely knocked her out – after the third I don't think she ate or moved for four days! But this was crucial in helping ensure Chris beat that initial short survival diagnosis. She had to have blood transfusions at this point to resolve her anaemia. The transfusions did their job, picked her back up and she resumed chemotherapy.

That was a very worrying week. Chris was so fragile I felt as though she was going to be gone in the next few weeks. She never complained but she was not her real self. I felt useless, unable to contribute anything to her situation.

We dealt with the future chemotherapy by assuming she would be poorly not on the day of treatment (she was normally fine), but for the next 3 days. Her curve was consistent: Okay-ish day 1, going downhill late that day, poorly day 2, slow recovery day 3, then okay.

We did this throughout the year, planned our holidays on that basis, booked lunches and days out on that basis and so on. By and large it worked perfectly. There was the odd hiccup – CT scan days were always bad news. Chris really struggled with these.

Chemotherapy dates:	February 19th
	February 26th
	March 5th
	March 19th
March 12th	Blood transfusion
March 13th	Consultant: Oncologist (Dr Mehra)
March 20th:	Consultant: Pancreas specialist (Dr Isaac)

Blood tests every Wednesday morning

21st March 2009 – Update No 3

We hope you are keeping well, and enjoying what appears to be the arrival of Spring. The daffodils are quite beautiful here in Worcestershire, snowdrops are now beginning to fade and there are signs of life on the buddleia and other trees.

Thanks to everybody for your enquiries and support over the last few weeks. We have both been really moved by the support given – the dietary ideas, the medical ideas, the spiritual support and many other things besides. These are the presents from our friends and family that are most appreciated and help us through the inevitable dark moments.

Chris continues to resist the whole concept of self pity. She is dealing with this in her usual calm, composed manner without histrionics but with inner strength. She carries with her great dignity, and deals with the whole thing on an 'I'll be alright'/'Let's see how it goes' basis. She has begun to lose her hair, and is now the 'proud' owner of a fancy new wig. This is a deeply emotional thing for the female, but once again Chris has dealt with it in her usual humorous way, mainly cursing the fact that her moulting hair could be from some bloody dog!

She has now had four treatments of chemotherapy. After three she was really knocked about, not eating for four days and was even weaker and more fatigued than before. After tests, it was established she was going anaemic and has had blood transfusions. As a result, the oncologist has reduced the strength of the dosage of gemcitabine.

She had her fourth treatment on Thursday, and so far has not been nearly as poorly as previously which we think is down to the reduced strength. We shall see. She even persuaded me to take her shopping for an hour in Worcester this afternoon, which actually proves she must be ill because that's the only reason I would ever take her shopping!

We have had some lovely trips out with our local friends, and visits from family members. If the reason for semi-retirement wasn't so awful, I could quite get used to this way of life!

Chris has her fifth treatment on Wednesday, then we head down to Cornwall – found a lovely hotel in Penzance – before taking a helicopter to Isles of Scilly on Thursday with Robert and family. We are both really looking forward to this week's holiday and hope that Chris will be ok with the travelling. We couldn't get her any insurance – quoted £1,700 for the week! – so, it's a bit of a gamble!

Alongside her treatment, we seem to have balanced out Chris's pain relief. She is on 'slow release' morphine (virtually everything else is not strong enough), but it does send her delightfully 'dippy' sometimes. Some things can be quite amusing, but the reality is that sometimes this 'dippy' person isn't my Chris at all and that tears into me somewhat in a very painful way.

Once we return it will only be a matter of days before our wonderful friend Debbie Hanfeld arrives from Australia. I will keep you updated on Chris's adventures with Debbie next month (believe me, when those two get together it means trouble!)

Meanwhile, thanks once again for your prayers and your thoughts. Keep them coming, as we continue to hope for a miracle from our Good Lord.

Love,
Chris & Trevor xxx

Hi Trevor,
Many thanks for this ... both Tina and I think of Chris, yourself and the family very often.

The reality of what has happened to our very dear friend Emma has now really started to hit home with both Tina and myself. Emma passed away and her funeral was last Thursday, a day that we and many, many others will never forget.

I truly admire Chris's grit and determination and I wish you all a splendid holiday together on the Isles of Scilly. There you will see the real joys of Spring that will give Chris so much pleasure. Please pass on our love and tell her of our thoughts for her.

Have a wonderful and delightful time,
Love Jeff & Tina (Hull) xx xx

We've got fingers, toes and everything else crossed in hoping that all goes marvellously well for you on your expedition to the Scillies. It was great to receive your e-mail, it makes such a difference to us that we can hear the latest news from time to time. There's hardly a day goes by without our wondering how you are are coping with the unavoidable demands of the medication regime.

Thinking of the Scilly Isles, there is clear evidence that people have lived there since neolithic times and although they didn't have Sikorsky helicopters, there's one thing that simply hasn't changed over thousands of years – the way that the arrival of spring brings a message of hope to all living creatures at the prospect of better times ahead. It's the kind of feeling we get when we see young children, daffodils and lambs. It's also the time when we move the clocks forward because the days are getting longer and we begin to notice the increasing power of the sun.

Whatever the actual weather is like next week, we hope that the sun will shine on you all.

With our love,
Val and Peter (Halman)

Hi Trev,
Thanks for the news.

As you know, Chris and you are in our prayers every night. Send her my love from one 'Dippie' person to another 'dippy' person.

God Bless,
Dave & Marilyn (Dippie)

Hi there Trev,
Thank you for the update on Chris – I hope she gets through Wednesday's treatment without too much discomfort. You are both in my prayers.

Shirl (Hunter)

I employed the marvellously maverick Shirley back in my BASF days. She is such a generous, warm hearted lady who I think still reckons she's really only 18. Her support during the year was great to receive.

Hi Trevor, thanks for the email.
Hilary was the same all the way through and such inner strength is amazing. It helps all those around too. We are thinking of you both.

Fond regards,
Clare (Farrands)

Hi to you both, thank you for keeping us up to date with Christine's progress Trevor. You are both in our thoughts every day, as are Robert and family. So glad to hear the dose of chemo has been weakened. I know we want to blast this thing into oblivion but we don't want Christine to go with it! I have heard that chemo can cause mouth ulcers. If Christine is suffering with these I recommend you get her some Adcortil in

Orabase. You can buy it over the counter at any chemist. It is a paste that starts the healing process doesn't just numb for half an hour like Bonjela. I was recommended it by a doctor years ago and wouldn't use anything else now. It's best applied at night as it does get rubbed off if you talk.

Look after each other and stay positive, the power of positive thought is an amazing thing. :-)

Lots of love,
Lesley, Dean James and Lewis (Carpenter)

Hi Trev & Chris,
What a beautiful moving update you have sent us Trevor, it does not surprise me how you report Chris's strength of character, this is one aspect of Chris that will always remain absolute and much stronger than many of us. God bless you both.

I am very intrigued about the wig, and would love to see photos, as you have me wondering, is it blond and curly or something more funky and Chris-like, ie blue or purple???? That would be Chris all over, being different. I do hope that you have a wonderful family time down in Cornwall, the helicopter flight sound terribly exciting; although I would not want to do it myself!!!! And to top it all after all of that, a visit from Debbie, how lovely, girlie chats, you know Trev you can't beat them! I think it will be off to the pub for you!

You still continue to have our love and prayers from our family. Chris is always in our prayers and in the next couple of weeks we have a special mass at our church for sick and loved ones. We take a fresh lily and put a little tag with the person's name on it. All the lilies are then placed around the church and we have a mass in honour of our loved ones. Sometimes the names are read out, and Chris's name will be amongst the group together with my sister.

Trevor, you must also make sure you are looking after yourself and getting some rest. Hopefully you are eating ok – but you're normally ok in that department?! Our thoughts are with you as well Trevor, and I hope that at some point you will let me know when I can come up and see you both.

June is coping well with her chemo and our family I think have never been closer. The Macmillan nurses should all be saints, as the support they give my sister and niece is just incredible. She is having an MRI again in 6 weeks, and this will tell us the status with the tumour.

In the meantime, we have had our ups and downs with our kids, but whilst this is challenging for us at this present time, is no comparison to what you both are going through.

Take good care, all our love, prayers and friendship.

God bless,
Sian & Mike, Conor, Alex and Jackson x x x (Ayckbourn)

I always refer to Sian as my 'adopted daughter. She has been a wonderful friend to us over the years, stemming back to when she was but a young girl when Chris suffered her aneurysm. Sian supported me down the phone through those dark days and she has been an important friend to us both since then. Her sister was fighting lung cancer in parallel with Chris's fight, so most of the time we spoke on the phone. Her husband Mike was always there for us if needed, they are truly part of our family.

25th April 2009

Hi,

Since Race For Life started Chris has taken part at the Worcester event, together with her great friend Sandra Jackson. Sadly, Chris's cancer makes it impossible for her to participate this year but her sister, Linda Brown, is taking her place and competing alongside Sandra. Linda is particularly keen to raise funds for Cancer Research because pancreatic cancer is terribly under-funded in research.

Linda has set up a donations webpage – this is the link http://www.raceforlifesponsorme.org/lindabrown4 - with donations going to Cancer Research

If you would like to support Linda in her support of Chris, please make your donations via the link.

Thanks for all your support, Chris has a scan on Monday and we get results on May 8th. I will update everybody after that.

Chris & I are both very grateful for any support you can give Linda.

Many thanks

Best wishes,
Trevor

Dear Trevor and Chris,

Thank you, Trevor, for the latest news on Christine's progress. I will continue to pray for her, of course. One realises every day, that one's small problems, which everyone has, are so minor, when one sees what Chris has to go through. I wish you both an enjoyable time, as circumstances allow, on your planned trip to Cornwall. I am sure that it will do you both good.

Love and best wishes,
Ulla (Pschierer)

Hello Trevor,

Just touching base to see how things are for you, how is Chris? last time we heard from you it was regarding very bad news. Please keep in touch.

All our love,
Paul, Monica and Charlotte xxx(Silver)

If I Should Fall Behind

~ Bruce Springsteen ~

Easter Monday - family get together at Isis (April 2009)

~ If I Should Fall Behind ~

Robert treated us to a week in the Isles of Scilly at the end of March.
Remember, we were working on a three/four month survival time so this was
an incredibly ambitious booking to make! This holiday with the family in the
Isles of Scilly was wonderful, very important in keeping the positive thoughts
flowing. Children are wonderful creatures. Oliver and Harriet spent the week
being devoted to their Granny, naturally aware (although all they knew was that
Granny was ill) that they needed to get in plenty of time with her. This inspired
Chris, who although pretty frail, dealt with them as she always did. The only
change was that she couldn't play 'tickle monster' with them in bed. Instead they
cuddled in and she passed on her wisdom to them by way of creative stories
with little anecdotes!

The Isles of Scilly (or at least Tresco) are wonderful. No cars, just walking, bikes
or for the ill, golf buggies at some excessive cost. The weather, terrible when
we arrived, improved to blue skies and warm sunshine. Bearing in mind Chris
had been so poorly just two weeks previously she was in fine form. Capable of
undertaking small amounts of walking, and fit enough to enjoy her halves of
lager, glasses of wine or gin and tonics, her enjoyment of spending time with
her favourite people was unbounded.

We all fussed around her (much to her displeasure, of course) making sure she
took plenty of rest. I have particularly fond memories of our one day alone.
Rob and family went off to St Marys and we hopped aboard the buggy to
explore. We called at the only pub for lunch, drove up to the tip of the island
(by the only hotel) and Chris sat on the beach in the sunshine. She looked
beautiful, obviously fragile and ill, but beautiful with her woolly pink hat on her
head to keep her warm. We held hands as we looked over the beach and sea. I
took a couple of photographs and wished we could stay forever.

It was idyllic on Tresco. It did wonders for Chris, confirming her view that she
could prove the doctor's timetable too pessimistic. She travelled in a helicopter
for the only time in her life, laughing at the noise with Ollie and Hattie. We
drove home happily, looking forward to the arrival the following week of
Debbie Hanfeld from Australia.

Debbie's arrival was unbelievably important for Chris. Deb had suffered tragedy in her own life, losing her husband Horst in 1998. Her visit was inspirational for Chris, and crucial in helping her live her miracle into 2010.

Debbie arrived for Easter. Her decision to visit Chris was a big positive in our 'miracle' strategy. They have been pals since 1988, Chris being a major supporter to Deb in London after she had given birth to her first son, Andy. Chris has been to visit Queensland half a dozen times, and I think she views Toowoomba as almost a second home. There were a lot of tears, mixed with laughter, on the evening of 9th April!

Before Deb's arrival I had decided that we should have a major family get-together on Easter Monday. A number of nieces and nephews wanted to visit Chris, but I felt they were a little scared of phoning to arrange because they were uncertain as to what the news might be. I hired a marquee for Easter Monday, sent out invitations by e-mail and by word of mouth, asking everybody to bring their own picnic and drink.

What a great day! The sun shone, the sky was blue, and Chris was in pretty good form. She was able to go into the house whenever she felt tired to rest (being Chris, this wasn't very often). She sat on the garden wall talking and laughing with everybody throughout the day. The children played cricket and football while the adults chatted. Debbie became acquainted with the Prices and the Loynes families as well as some of our closest friends.

This day was one of my best decisions of the year. Everyone would now remember Auntie Chris from how she was that day. Not as a sick person who died of cancer, but a beautiful, laughing, amusing woman in control of herself and her life. This is important. I personally struggled for several months after Chris died to take my memory beyond Chris's last 18 days spent in hospital. I blamed myself for not having her admitted to hospital quicker, for not insisting on a head scan, for not cancelling our final cruise in order that she could have her lung drained - in fact, for everything I could possibly think of I blamed myself. This is, of course, stupid but it didn't stop me doing it.

But because this was such a happy day, most of the family and our close friends only have these good memories to recall.

Later that week we set off with Debbie for 5 days in North Devon. Once again, like Tresco, the weather was excellent. Not baking hot (it was only April), but blue skies and sunshine. Woolacombe Bay Hotel is a fine example of a terrific English seaside hotel – good service, well furnished rooms, great food. We had a two-bedroom suite (I refer you to my life assurance comments!) that enabled Chris to take rest whenever she needed without disturbing us.

We had a lovely few days, exploring North Devon both on foot (Chris was able to walk about half a mile most days) and in the car. Chris and Deb had lots of time together, which was important for them both. Although we all prayed for a different result, this proved to be their final time together as friends.

Debbie's visit was the true confirmation that visitors gave Chris something to look forward to and, in forming objectives for us both, were key in our battle.

Visitors gave Chris a reason to make an effort. It is too easy when you are so sick to never get dressed, never put on your make-up, never attempt to look glamorous. Visitors make you do these things. Chris wanted to look good, wanted to be well, didn't want to use her wheelchair. All these constituted positive things; all helping her mental strength. Visitors also brought fresh topics of conversation. When you're together 24 hours a day it is very easy to run out of conversation – we needed inspiration!

Debbie left us on 22nd April and headed for Dublin. She had been a real inspiration for Chris, and I found myself hoping that the let-down after she had gone would not be too great for her. I needn't have worried, Chris was made of sterner stuff. Plus, we had now given ourselves other trips to look forward to. A strategy of targeted incentives and objectives had now become set in stone – we would follow this route whatever people thought (and some thought we were slightly mad and over optimistic).

The full confirmation of this was that I booked a two week cruise for us on the Queen Victoria, in their Grills (virtually 1st Class) for the end of July. It never entered my head that Chris would not survive past six months. We were rolling!

Chemotherapy: *April 3rd*
                    April 16th
                    April 23rd
                    May 7th

April 27th   *CT Scan:*

Blood tests every Weds

May 8th   *Consultant: Oncologist (Dr Mehra)*

Hi to you both,

Just wanted to say thanks for a lovely day on Monday. It was great to see everybody again and also to meet some of Aunty Christine's family. The kids had a great time, and it was nice to see so many kids that didn't know each other getting along. We hope you're having a relaxing time in Devon and look forward to seeing you both again later in the year, if Aunty Christine feels up to it.

All our love,

Lesley, Dean, James and Lewis Xxx (Carpenter)

Trev,

Just wanted to say thanks for organising and hosting Monday's get-together. I think everyone had a really great time - we certainly did. Hope it wasn't too much for Chris. I've attached a nice photo that I took on the day.

Cheers, Nick & family. (Brown)

8th May 2009 – Update No 4

Hi

Hope all is well with you. Since my last bulletin Chris has encountered both the good and the bad with her illness. Her appetite has veered from good to non-existent, and her physical condition from reasonable (walking) to having to use her wheelchair for the first time. The chemotherapy has taken 90% of her hair, but she seems utterly unfazed by it! We've got her morphine painkillers down to only 30mg per 24hrs, which means she is less 'high/out of it' during the day, which is a great development.

Inevitably I managed to pass my cough to Chris, which meant that her blood count went down and she couldn't have any chemotherapy last week. She was ok this week and has had another bout of chemotherapy yesterday. Also, last week, she had her first scan since diagnosis.

Her scan has brought us some really encouraging news. Her tumour has been reduced, there are no signs of spread to her lymphs and the slight tumour in her liver has been eliminated – so although the chemotherapy is really awful (you wouldn't wish it on your worst enemy), it is doing the job. We are both relieved at this news from the oncologist, which we received today after her scan. We now have to resolve her current problems with her legs and life will be a little more enjoyable for her.

We have been away on holiday a couple of times. Towards end of March we went to the Isles of Scilly (Tresco) with Robert and family. We had a lovely time and Chris thoroughly enjoyed herself. She coped well with both the long journey down to Penzance as well as helicopter journeys to and from, and whilst she was off colour over the weekend (as she normally is after chemotherapy), she generally ate well and was able to do a little walking when we visited the gardens at Tresco Abbey.

Debbie (Hanfeld) arrived from Australia on 9th April, and her visit really picked Chris up. We had a week at home, which included the family get together on Easter Monday, before heading off to North Devon to stay at Woolacombe for 5 nights. Again, Chris coped well with the journey down and also managed a little walking over the holiday. She was pretty poorly on the Sunday but otherwise, as we were blessed with fine weather, we were able to enjoy the sunshine in the hotel gardens. Chris ate well and she and Deb gave the bar a bashing on the Friday evening!

Deb left for Ireland and London on 22nd, before returning to Australia last weekend. We miss her. Chris loves to have visitors – I can be really boring, believe me – and so if you would like to visit please drop an email, or give a ring, and we'll arrange a date. We have further holiday plans made as we believe it's important to keep having things to which to look forward, so for Chris, together with her Mum and sisters, it's Mid Wales at the end of May while I take my seat in front of the telly to watch United take on Barcelona!

Thanks for all the messages and particular thanks to all who have supported Linda on the 'Race for Life'. Your support has brought her nearly £1,000 sponsorship in Chris's name which is utterly overwhelming. http://www.raceforlifesponsorme.org/lindabrown4

God Bless

Trevor

xxx

Hi Trev,

That's very good news and I hope we can see you on May 16/17. The balloon flight is at 6.30 am on Saturday weather permitting. I am not sure when it will finish, but I would expect to be free by midday. Could we drop over in the afternoon maybe?

All the best and look forward to seeing you both.
Rowl (Charge)

Rowl and I go back 50 years to our schooldays at Kings, Worcester. We shared a love of music and mayhem reflected by our rather irreverent view of the world, something we continue to share to this day. Rowl is a fabulous chum, utterly reliable as a friend while appearing slightly to live his life in an exotic, airy-fairy cloud, slightly distant from the real world.

Hi Trevor,

It's always good to hear from you, and to learn how Chris is progressing.

Marilyn and I have just returned from a week in Bodmin. We visited the Eden project, as well as St Ives, Mevagissey, Boscastle, Padstow and Tintagel.

You are both in our prayers, and we always have a bed for you in Poynton.

God Bless,
D & M (Dippie)

Hello Trevor,

I am so pleased to hear your encouraging news and hope Chris goes on to successfully beat this dreadful disease.

It sounds as though Chris has the right attitude and a strong determination, this together with a loving family and friends around her I am sure she will pull through this. It may take time and be horribly painful at times but as long as she stays with us that is the main thing.

Our love and best wishes to you both.
Liz and Sean (Forde) xx

Liz worked for me at Emtec, a gentle, honest human being who always brought a positive into our lives. It was lovely to hear from her and know they were part of Chris's army of support.

Thanks for the update, I am so glad there is some good news, fingers, toes, everything crossed that the improvements continues.

Sounds like Chris isn't going to let this cancer beat her, keep going love, give it hell, haha.

Love,
Mandy & family x (Cottle)

Well done Chris, chemo is pretty awful but you seems to be coping. You continue to be in our thoughts and prayers.

Clare (Farrands)

Hi Trevor,
Very pleased to have your e-mail and learn that Chris is doing well, it was very welcome news on the scan front.

We have been to Lesley's for a week to be there for Lewis's birthday on the Sunday. He was 7 and growing up fast.

We shall look forward to hearing how Linda gets on with the race, £1000 is worth running for.

Love to you both,

God Bless,
Rosemary and Jim (Allan)
xxx

Hi,
Fabulous news from the specialist, really pleased to hear that the treatment is having a positive effect. Would be great to pop in and see you both, will send over some dates when we are passing nearby and we can call in for a cuppa and catch up.

Have a great time in Wales Chris... and enjoy the Barcelona game Trev, just how pleasing was it to see Drogba at the final whistle!!!

Love to all,
Paul & Sue (Blake)

Dear Trev,
What wonderful news! I am delighted to hear of Chris's inner strength continuing to

help her defy gravity! She is certainly made of strong stuff and thank heavens for it.

I'm slightly under the weather myself, but hope to be able to set worries aside following a day of colonoscopy and endoscopy tomorrow and a chat with the consultant on Friday.

I really am pleased to hear your news, and may it continue to be more up than down for you both.

Yours aye,
Tony (Wightman)

Tony and I met almost twenty years ago when we used his ad agency at BASF. We shared a love of good restaurants, fine wine and excessive expense accounts! But out of our terrible abuse of the company's money grew real friendship, Chris got to know him as well and we have met up on a regular basis over the years. Tony has suffered his own tribulations, but these never were in the way of giving Chris his unswerving support during the year.

Thank you, Trevor, for the latest report on Chris. I was pleased to read the 'good news' about her treatment. It must be dreadful. I really admire her. However, having you at her side, must help a great deal as you have always been an optimist, smiling, rather than moaning. I will continue to pray for Chris, that's all I can do. I am glad that you are managing a few breaks – that's marvellous.

Just before I close, I want to pass on a special message to you and Chris: Nell Leach, I used to work with for many years; in fact, I interviewed and employed her at Gillespie Road, the Chapel near Arsenal Station. She was dealing with special accounts. I expect that you, Trevor, will remember her. I can't think how old she and Derek, her husband, are today? She writes to me at Christmas and birthday, always looking at the bright side in life. Anyway, I thought I would pass her best wishes on to you both.

Love,
Ulla (Pschierer)

Trevor,
Thank you for keeping us posted. Chris has been in our thoughts and spoken of in despatches recently.

Fantastic news on the treatment it's encouraging to know that it's having some impact. We hope that she continues to make good progress. Let's hope that we have a good summer where Chris can take advantage of the weather.

Sending love and best wishes to you both,
Sharon & Tim (Woolridge)

Hi Trev,
Please wish Chris all the best from Karen and myself. It's good to hear that she is so positive – it is her best strategy – never accept what they tell you, it's up to you. We lost a friend last year who defied the odds (given to her by the medics) by more than three years – she was very courageous as Chris is being.Trevor, if there is anything that I can do to help you know that you only have to ask.

Our thoughts are with you, Chris and Robert and his family.

Take care my friend.

All the best,
John (Frost)

John and I met when I tutored at The Leadership Trust. He was my course director on several occasions. Since then he mentored my Emtec management team and became a close and important friend to me. We had dinners with him and Karen down in Ross on Wye. John has been a source of strength for many years to me, and also integral to the development of my business (and life) values over the years.

Hello Trevor and Christine,
Good news, please God let it carry on being good and you can have a bit of enjoyment over our promised summer months. We would love to come and see you both and will ring to see if you are in. We have been travelling a lot in our little motor home. Dickie has got the bug for it. I have been doing a lot of gardening and the gardens front and back look lovely. We had a lovely day with Brenda and Brian yesterday, Brenda loved a chicken pie I made for their lunch. Please give our love to everyone, Sandra and Malcolm, Stepha and Brian, etc. We do miss you all but not the company or the pressures any more. Dickie hasn't got to go back to the doctors for six months and looks younger than I have seen him look in years. He even sunbathes now which he never ever did before. Please tell Chris we are praying for her and will keep her in our thoughts.

Lots of love,
Chrissy and Dickie (Probert)

Trevor and Chris,

Thank you for the update. I have been away last week to see my daughter and grandson in the Isle of Man and a reunion with old flat mates (40 years ago) and some golf, and like Trevor ended up with some bug, so I am trying to catch up at work with everything.

Good luck with the chemo Chris and thinking of you both.
Kevin (Fay)

Hi to you both. We are all so glad to here the chemo is doing the job and zapping those tumours. It must have given you both such a boost to hear such encouraging news. Our thoughts continue to be with you every day and we are looking forward to hearing more good news soon. We hope you have some good quality girl time in Wales with your Mum and sister and look forward to hearing all about it.

Lots of love as always,
Lesley, Dean and boys (Carpenter)

Hi,

It's good to hear that Chris is coping with all the treatment. We are thinking of you. Gord is still out of work, doctor will not let him go back yet so i have been working extra hours so I don't get a lot of time to read my emails but you are always in our hearts. Hope to see you soon.

Lots of love,
Jackie (Callow)

After Chris's latest chemotherapy on May 7th she began to develop the first signs of troubles with her legs. They began to be sore, feeling heavy and tender to the touch. We treated with cream and she had further chemotherapy on May 21st before setting out on holiday to Llandridod Wells on May 26th with her Mum and two sisters.

Reports are that the four days were enjoyable, despite the problems with her legs. I'm uncertain as to weather conditions, but these days were important. They were to be the last days they spent as a family group, so it was probably even more important to her Mum.

May 21st   Chemotherapy

June 17th   Dexa scan:

17th June 2009

Further to my email on 25th April, I am delighted to report that Chris's sister Linda completed the Race For Life in Worcester last Sunday. She and Sandra (Jackson) completed in 55 minutes, a very commendable effort.

What has been so amazing is the quite fantastic support Linda received from you all. Her original target for Cancer Research was set at £100. Just on her Race For Life webpage - http://www.raceforlifesponsorme.org/lindabrown4 - you good friends have given £1135. In addition, I personally have another £100 committed to collect and I know that Linda has a similar amount.

Chris and I would like to thank you so much. We are both deeply moved by your support, and the kind messages you put on the webpage and sent to us. It is impossible to explain how much this has meant to us. Needless to say, the webpage is still 'open for business' if you missed the earlier opportunity! http://www.raceforlifesponsorme.org/lindabrown4 .

Chris is doing better than we could expect. She has passed the first survival time-frame given us (four months) and is now set upon beating the pancreatic average (9 months) in October. She has good and bad days, and has been confined to a wheelchair for the past four/five weeks with reaction to chemotherapy, although her legs are now much better after no chemotherapy for four weeks. She expects to start treatment again next week. We've had a holiday each month and these have helped, and we have a couple more planned for next week and late July.

Thank you once again, words cannot express how much this has helped us.

Take Care – Live The Dream,
Trevor & Chris

That's wonderful news, Trevor. I am a great believer in the power of prayer and positive thinking, and it is so good to know that Chris is fighting back. May I add her name to our prayer list at church? I wouldn't like to do so without your permission.

Best wishes to you both,
Rosemary (Allan)

Trevor,
I am so touched with your email. I am delighted how much Chris has raised. Well done to you as well for helping to raise such a fantastic amount.

I am glad to hear that you are both having holidays and Chris really is an inspiration to us all.

Take care and God bless you both.

Kind regards.
Sue xx (White) – Marie Curie

Great to hear a milestone has passed and Chris is surviving with some dignity, humour and sometimes even bloody mindedness. You must be feeling the strain and it is easy to say but our thoughts and prayers are with you both. Each day must have its ups and downs and you are constantly aware of the fragile peace you have. Every day Chris is here means God is preparing a really cool setup and he can wait as long as it takes. We very sincerely hope she can make the Guinness Book of Records.

'Many O' them',
John (Oliver)

Hi Trev,
Cheque went into the post tonight - honest!! I've addressed it to you rather than try to catch up elsewhere.

Although trying to keep up to date with Chris's situation by your e-mail, I know I should have rang you - please put it down to not having over positive news at this end, coupled with not wanting to 'get in the way' and being relatively busy away from home, as a complicated set of reasons or an awful excuse - your choice!

Please be assured you both are constantly in my thoughts.

All the best for now,
Ken (Lewis)

Dear Trevor and Chris
Val and I have just been re-reading your fourth report on Chris's treatment and how you're all coping with a very challenging situation.

I think it would be entirely accurate to say that the way in which you two are dealing with the problems is simply inspirational. We've known you for rather more than a year or two and have always admired your totally positive approach to the hand of cards you've been dealt. Shining through everything else has been your love for and commitment to your family. In our opinion, a happy and thriving family is far more important than all the houses, money, cars, holidays or designer labels. Yes, Trevor, even more important than your beloved Man Utd! You two are an example to everyone who knows you and even if it makes you blush, feel free to feel proud of what you've created.

If only there were something practical we could do to help. It's not much, but all we can offer is our love and support. We think about you every day and look forward to hearing some further positive news from our dearest friends in the Bewdley Brigade.

With our love
Val and Peter (Halman)

With Debbie Hanfeld at The Woolacombe Bay Hotel, and the usual gin and tonics!

Goin' Back

~ Dusty Sprinfield ~

Carole, Robert and Chris on the Lleyn Peninsula, North Wales (June 2009)

~ Goin' Back ~

At our consultation with liver specialist Dr Isaac, he tells us that unless we have some specific reasons to see him he doesn't feel we need to waste our time coming up to Birmingham. He feels that our oncologist is 'on top of the case', and that as surgery is not an option the inconvenience to us is too great to make it a worthwhile visit for us. Chris is relaxed with this.

By now, I was ensuring her mother was regularly a weekend visitor because I felt it was important for her to spend time with her youngest daughter. For a mother to lose a child must be so terrible as to be beyond understanding. I wanted to make sure they had plenty of time together, to have a really long farewell opportunity.

We had some terrific weekends together throughout the year. Chris's mum is a truly exceptional woman. The pair of them sat and talked the day (and night) away. I had joined us in a DVD film club so that Chris always had something to watch if she became a little bored with her Sudoku or there were no visitors around. Mum sat watching them with us, amused by the bad language in some of them. My cooking improved with two experts present to help, and Chris helped me drink the bottles of wine from the collection we had always purchased together on our visits to France.

Late June we set off with Chris's brother Robert, and wife Carole, for a three day trip revisiting their childhood holiday places on the Lleyn Peninsula in North Wales. This was a great trip. Chris had a truly special relationship with Rob. I had the feeling this was a very important three days for them both, reliving special childhood memories that I am not privileged to know. Chris was radiant, although weak, during these days. She was walking better, the weather yet again was beautiful for her and it was a pleasure to be alive.

Our hotel was lovely, the dining spectacular. It was so great to see Chris enjoy her food. She simply never let her chemotherapy treatment destroy that enjoyment.

We visited all those special childhood places and, as always, I was regaled with their childhood stories. Learning to drive on the campsite, shivering on cold days on Whistling Sands, playing in the garden at The Red Lion, their Dad going fishing at night with Uncle Ron, playing in the cafe at Aberdaron

- and many more that brought the twinkle back into Chris's eyes. This was the real pleasure for me - to see her twinkle restored, even though it was only temporary. Her eyes had somehow become sadder after she had been diagnosed, they had lost a little of life's sparkle. These trips - and especially these memories - brought back her smiles and the laughter that were an integral part of her personality.

We walked down to the beaches at Aberdaron, Llanbedrog and Nefyn, where we sat on the steps and reminisced. Lovely memories for Chris on her last visit to favourite places. After her death, the three of us returned to the peninsula. We climbed the headland and scattered some of her ashes there, overlooking Llangwnnadi beach and out to the Atlantic. Chris will rest easy there, a smile on her face and her eyes laughing in the sunlight as she oversees all future generations playing on those golden sands.

Chris's brother, Robert, was one of the pillars upon which we built our miracle. Our son Robert, his wife Pippa and the grand-children were others. Dave and Marie Grandison. Sandra Jackson. Individuals who loved Chris beyond words, and who supported everything we did even if they thought we were being just a bit over optimistic. Brother Robert arrived most weekends on his Triumph motor-bike to visit Chris, bringing gifts and spending hours talking with her, encouraging her and helping her realise how loved she was by her family.

At times like these the whole cancer thing seemed just a bad dream. How could this vibrant, wonderful woman be slowly dying in front of my eyes? As we sat eating dinner in the wonderful hotel restaurant I wanted to scream at God that he was unjust and unfair, that he should give us our miracle cure and let this so-good person live her full term. I have never liked unfairness and this was unfair.

We returned to Chris's first chemotherapy for four weeks, followed by a nuclear body scan at City Hospital, Birmingham. Not a good experience. Chris was off the pace, really very poorly indeed that day and having to use the wheelchair. The place was depressing and we were pleased to just get out alive to return home to our spoilt, quiet country life.

June 26th   Chemotherapy:

June 29th   Nuclear Body Scan:

1st July 2009 – Update No 5

Hi

Hope everything is going well in your world.

Since my last bulletin on 16th May, Chris has had a mixed time with everything.

At the end of May, she went off on a few days holiday with her two sisters and her Mum to Llandrindod Wells. Although by then her walking difficulties were beginning to seriously affect her, all reports are that a good time was had by all. Unfortunately, as June progressed the side-effects from her chemotherapy became more pronounced in her legs. She was in constant pain – she could barely touch them they were so tender – and could just about walk ten yards at most. She had to deal with being in a wheelchair, which she dealt with in her usual practical way despite the obvious psychological problems. She is so very brave.

When we saw the oncologist on June 5th he immediately decided no more treatment for another two weeks (making four in all) in an attempt to relieve her legs. Over the month she has improved, the pain lessened and she was able to walk again (not a long distance but significantly more than ten yards). We took a trip with Chris's brother and wife up to the Lleyn Peninsula in North Wales last week, and we had a wonderful time. It picked Chris up loads, and she came back with a nice suntan and in good heart to resume treatment last Friday.

Sadly, resuming treatment has knocked her about badly. Added to her treatment, she has had to have a couple of bone scans and yesterday a new CT scan because the doctor is concerned she may have a blood clot. She has had severe chest pains, and now these have moved down to her liver area in the last 48 hours which is very concerning. She is also sleeping more again, although this may be as a result of increasing her morphine pain killing tablets.

Chris has two more planned weeks of chemotherapy – which is something not to be welcomed – but we hope that it will once again have positive effects on the cancer. Let's hope the bone scans and blood clot checks are positive. She will then have a week off any treatment (we hope!) before we go on our big adventure on July 20th – a two week cruise around the Mediterranean on the Queen Victoria. Chris has been looking forward to this, and in her wheelchair we've been shopping around Worcester for her new clothes.

So, in summary I guess things have been as we'd expect. We take everyday as it comes, pray for a miracle and dream that, having beaten our first survival target of four months (the original diagnosis) we now will beat the second target of October.

Thank you for your kindness and support, so important to us both.

God bless,
Trevor & Chris xxx

Oh dear Trevor
I am so sorry Chris is going through all this – your heart must be broken. I know she is a brave and strong lady and will beat your October figure.

Have fun on your cruise in July which is this month now I guess.

Please keep your spirits up – I wish there was some way I could help.

Kindest regards,
Shirley (Hunter)

PS I am on Facebook now and just returned from a trip to the UK. If you have a moment please take a look.

Hugs to you both, sooo jealous you are going on a cruise, enjoy!

Mandy & family x (Cottle)

Dear Trevor,
Deb and I were heartbroken to hear about Chris.

We have been terrible in keeping in touch with you over the last several years. For that we are very sorry. Please let us know if there is anything we can do during this very difficult time.

We hope that your cruise is filled with a great deal of joy and happiness. Chris is blessed to have you and Robert in her life.

Please know that you will all be in our thoughts and prayers.

With warmest regards,
Gary and Debbie (Murrish)

Gary & Debbie live in Los Angeles. They'e been friends since our first visit to see Geoff (Owens) over there in 1983. We have laughed long into the night with them and it was wonderful to be back in touch with them after some lost years.

Dear Trevor,

Words cannot express how sad I feel reading your e-mail. I just don't know what to say, other than 'we are thinking of you both, and pray for the best'.

Maybe it is a small comfort to know that you are not alone etc. Sorry, but it's all I can say. Take care of yourselves.

Best wishes,
Gary & Carol.(Milner)

Hi to you both.
Love from us all. Thanks for the updates. It helps to know how things are progressing.

Only 2+ weeks to your adventure.

God bless you both.
D & M (Dippie)

Thanks for the update.

We can only 'watch' from the sidelines as you both exist through each day - but it does help us to know that in spite of everything you are so upbeat.

Chris has had such a rotten time and this awful disease does not treat people kindly. The pain is the most hellish effect and it is all right smiling bravely but sometimes she just has to scream.

We will be thinking about you on your voyage and when you come back we would dearly love to meet up wherever we can.

Take great care both of you,
John and Florence (Oliver)

Thanks Trevor - we are away for two weeks but I hope that Chris does the very best she possibly can.

X Tim (Kidson)

Dear Chris and Trevor
I am deeply moved by this email and my admiration for Chris in particular and both of you is beyond measure. Have a fantastic time on the cruise and be as great for each other as I know you will.

With love and best wishes,
Tony (Mills)

god bless to you both

netty and julian xxxxx
ps can I drop in on my way back home up long bank!
Julian (Turner)

Hello Trev & Chris,
Thanks for the update - obviously it is very distressing to hear of the reaction to the
chemo. It is impossible to imagine what you are going through. Just keep thinking
about the Mediterranean cruise, Chris... and right after that we are coming to see you
(probably August 10th) so you'd better be in good shape for that. Keep praying for the
miracle - they do happen, you know. Love to you both - we will see you soon.

Geoff (Owens)

Hi there,
Chris is more than brave... I know. I hope you enjoy the cruise and I pray your souls
will retain their peace.

Clare (Farrands)

You are an inspiration, the pair of you. And very often in my thoughts.

Much love and admiration,
Sue (Richardson)

Sue is a business friend from my networking events days.

Hi Trev and Chris
Thanks Trev for keeping us up-to-date on events on your side of the world. It sounds,
Chris, like you are having mixed fortunes. Although you were having difficulties
walking, I imagine it was great to get away with your Mum and sisters to the Welsh
countryside. Of course, where you live, it makes sense that you take a few trips to
Wales as it is only a couple of hours away. There's nothing like you Brits. We do our
best these days to avoid the sun (and sun tan/burn), but give you lot a couple of
spare days, and you're off to get a tan in North Wales.

The chemo sounds awful. I wish there was something anyone could do to relieve
the effects. It maybe OK as long as it gives you some better days. We look forward

to hearing news that the CT scan shows some benefits of the trials you have had to endure. Remember, it's just over two weeks until the Queen Vic cruise. That will be brilliant! Where do you go? I imagine Majorca, various Italian ports and the Greek islands? Maybe somewhere in North Africa? You should get a look at the sun anyway.

We are all about the same here. Retirement is wonderful, even if it means taking on the Deputy Chair of a private school on the Sunshine Coast (I must admit that the position has a useful stipend attached to it) and doing some consulting work (albeit to help set up a sports academy on the Gold Coast). Between these things and doing a lot of building, painting and decorating, I don't know how I had time to work.

We had quite a surprise last weekend. Simon finished his apprenticeship as a builder and so we took he and Rachel out for a few drinks and dinner that night. As we were leaving, Simon told me that he'd be over to our place next morning as he had a venture to discuss with me. I fully expected that that meant borrowing money, so next morning I asked him what he might need the money for? A bit timidly, he announced that he needed to buy an engagement ring, which he duly went ahead and acquired with the assistance (and great jubilation) of his mother. Subsequently, Rachel said 'yes' and so we have the prospect of a wedding somewhere in the future. We're quite happy about this as Rachel is a wonderful match for Simon. She's a Kiwi, but we have forgiven her for that.

Chris, keep on keeping on. We think of you and your trials all the time. As the fighter we know you are, we're sure that you can make the next goal, which is to have a wonderful time on the Mediterranean cruise. We look forward to hearing a report of your adventures.

Fondest regards
Laurie and Linda (Vogler)

Dear Trevor and Chris,
Thank you very much for your latest report. I do admire Chris for her positive outlook, and also you, but you have always been looking at the bright side in life, even when business problems arose; do you remember the time with Bert Smits? I certainly have not forgotten as to what I had to endure with him. His German was bad. He insisted in spelling every word with 'small' letters!!

I can well imagine that Chris could suffer badly after chemo. Anyway, all your various breaks must have helped both of you. I do hope that the Med Cruise will help you both to cope with the problem.

I now thank God for every day I am given. I shall continue praying for Chris, and wish you both all the best.

Ulla (Pschierer)

PS: I don't know whether I told you that Nell sends her best wishes too.

Hi Trev,

Thanks for sending this update. I really admire the courage that you are both showing in dealing with this and I wish you all the best for the 'big adventure'.

We are on vacation from tomorrow 5th to 19th so will probably not speak again before you go so have a great adventure.

Take care both of you,

John (Frost)

Hello Trevor,

Thank you for those nice piccies, as you call them. I must say, you have not changed at all and Chris does not look too bad. She does not even look thin, just nice and slim. What a lovely countryside you stayed at - very peaceful looking. There is too much noise everywhere these days.

Carry on both of you being brave - time will tell.

Best wishes,

Ulla (Pschierer)

Hi to you both.

What a wonderful job Christine's sister did of, 1. completing the race and 2. raising so much money. it was a pleasure to donate to such a worthy cause. Sorry to hear that Christine is having a rough time at the moment. I have spoken to Mum and she let me know that Christine is much better following the blood clot scare which was a great relief to hear. I hope you enjoyed their visit last weekend, it is good that they are close enough to just stay one night and not intrude on your privacy too much. Have Robert and Pippa been getting up as often as possible? Seeing the children must give Christine such a boost. We hope you have a fantastic time on your cruise and look forward to hearing all about it when you get back. Well that's all for now. please remember we think of you both everyday and send you all our love and positive thoughts.

Lesley, Dean, James and Lewis. xxxxxx

Hi Trevor,

You perhaps don't remember me from early BASF days, but I was visiting Bill Ward yesterday and he showed me a copy of a rather distressing letter you had sent to Peter Fincham re the problems with your wife Chris. I'm naturally very sorry to hear that the future is not too bright but at least you appear to be making the best use of your time together.

Both Bill and myself have gone through the traumas of this disease, under completely different circumstances, but I know what you both must be going through at this very stressful time.

I believe you might be away on your cruise at present, enjoying the sea air and sun (hopefully) so there is a chance you will not get this email for a week or two.

I'm now retired but because of our 'leader' stealing most of my pension, I continue to do some work for a couple of organisations and have just been asked to give a couple of specialist lectures to a group of university students, which makes me tremble with fear.

The treatment I received here in Bedford and Cambridge for my cancer was absolutely brilliant and I now drive, once a week, radio therapy patients from this area to Addenbrookes in Cambridge. You might be interested to learn this is a unique service, as the vehicles (4) are owned by the Macmillan and Hospital Trust, fuelled by a local radio and TV dealer and run by volunteers. The patients are telephoned the night before and given a pick-up time and there is no waiting around after treatment for some obscure driver who might or might not arrive. It's just a pity that this service is not nationwide!

You might or might not know that Peter Fincham lost his younger daughter a few months ago, which has caused him and his wife Margaret great distress, so do not be surprised if you don't get a reply to your letter just yet. They still do not know the cause of death which is very distressing to them both.

I hope you don't mind me contacting you, but I thought you might like a little support.

Kindest regards,
Nick Ward

Mr Tambourine Man

~Bob Dylan ~

Chris looked so beautiful and was so happy on the Queen Victoria cruise (July 2009) it was difficult to realise that she was on a 'ticking clock'.

With our wonderful fellow travellers on Table 132, Princess Grill on Queen Victoria, a trip of a lifetime - from the left: Margaret, Albie, Miriam, John, Betty, Trevor, Chris & John (July 2009)

~ Mr Tambourine Man ~

Many years ago (1993) Chris and I visited Australia for the first time. On the way (and back) we stopped off at some Pacific Islands. On our way home we visited Fiji, then took a galleon (I kid you not!) to a tiny place offshore called Beachcomber Island. You could walk around Beachcomber in five minutes, it really was that small. There we met backpackers galore, lay on soft sands under blue skies and understood how blessed we were. We were only there three nights, and on our last night after a wonderful evening of storytelling and friendship we headed towards our beds at about two o'clock in the morning, needless to say somewhat the worse for alcohol.

On arriving at our beach house (bure), we undressed but instead of climbing into bed we wandered hand in hand, absolutely naked apart from a walkman with a cassette tape, into the sea. The stars were utterly beautiful, the moon gorgeous, the night a beautiful temperature and then we sat in the warm sea together. We both put our headphones on and I played Bob Dylan's 'Mr Tambourine Man'. This song contains these wonderful words in the last verse:

> Then take me disappearin' through the smoke rings of my mind
> Down the foggy ruins of time, far past the frozen leaves
> The haunted, frightened trees, out to the windy beach
> Far from the twisted reach of sorrow
> Yes, to dance beneath the diamond sky with one hand waving free
> Silhouetted by the sea, circled by the circus sands
> With all memory and fate driven deep beneath the waves
> Let me forget about today until tomorrow
>
> Hey! Mr. Tambourine Man, play a song for me
> I'm not sleepy and there is no place I'm going to
> Hey! Mr Tambourine Man, play a song for me
> In the jingle jangle morning I'll come followin' you

During these minutes Chris and I were in a place together that was so special, so beautiful and so important that words between us weren't needed. We sat, listening to our hero singing these wonderful, indescribable words to us knowing we were living the very words he had written. We really were dancing under the diamond sky.

I relate this story to try to explain our cruise in July, to try to help place its importance in our life together. Beachcomber lived with us for ever, we talked about it forever. Our cruise on Queen Victoria assumed the same level of importance.

July had brought us into Chris's seventh month since diagnosis. It also brought us towards this major holiday of 2009 or any other year. When I booked our Mediterranean cruise I did so as a way to give Chris a real major target to aim at, something to help keep her positive and challenged. In the weeks leading up to it she sorted out her clothes, and I took about three car-loads to our local charity shop for Kemp House hospice. I insisted Chris have, basically, a brand new wardrobe for the trip. I wanted her to look a million dollars, not like someone who was terminally ill.

With her wonderful short hair and her new outfits she looked as radiant as I've ever seen her. Actually, I didn't realise at the time how much she was looking forward to the cruise. She told lots of her visitors, but never told me. She probably didn't want to over excite me. Our photographs show a lady at ease with her condition, not feeling resentful; someone refusing to accept her death but comfortable knowing it was slowly happening. By now, after seven months, I was used to Chris's responses to being asked how she was – 'I'm alright', was always her reply. Chris never did self-pity.

It was a most wonderful trip. We met some wonderful people. Our dining table was blessed with three of the most wonderful couples you could care to meet. The treatment we received in the Princess Grill (Cunard's Business Class is the easiest way to describe it) was perfect.

We made no secret of Chris's condition. We told our fellow diners on the first night that we were there because Chris was dying. They were so supportive of her and we were proud to call them our friends by the end of the trip.

The trip I had booked was chosen because (1) it was no-fly, (2) it fitted in with Chris's week off during the chemotherapy programme and (3) the weather should be hot. Her oncologist was totally supportive of this holiday (and all the others). We saw him immediately before we set off to Southampton to confirm he was okay with Chris's condition for her to travel. I went with enough medication to keep a small hospital stocked, although was reassured that there were doctors and nurses on board if required.

This trip was the highlight of our final year together. We were closer as a couple than ever, knowing just by a glance or a look what the other was thinking. We held each other so close and I think we both felt that it could never, ever get any better than this. There was no beach, no warm sea, no naked dancing but it was our diamond sky in 2009 where we were able to forget about today until tomorrow.

Chemotherapy:

July 10th
August 7th

July 17th

Consultant: Oncologist (Dr Mehra)

7th August 2009 – Update No 6

Hi,
Hope everything is well with you. Bit of a long report!

Since my last update things have continued to go well for Chris, and of course we've been away on our cruise. I've attached a couple of photos from the cruise on Queen Victoria to show how well Chris is doing.

As you are aware, our reason for the cruise was very much Chris's health issue (and her potential short period left with us here), and she thoroughly enjoyed the two weeks. With her prognosis, I take the view that by constantly setting positive targets for the future (such as holidays) it helps her to fight the bad times when she is receiving chemotherapy treatment. We know that her condition is incurable, but we also know that unless you strive for 'the miracle' it won't happen!

We had a wonderful time. Chris remained fighting fit the whole trip and there is little doubt the sunshine had a very positive effect. As you can see, she looks a million dollars – you'd never believe she is so ill.

We met some lovely people, particularly at our Dinner Table 132. John and Margaret from Nottinghamshire were on their forty-something cruise celebrating their golden wedding (plus John's 74th birthday). Amazingly they have seen the world from the QE2 – 25 cruises! Albie and Miriam were an American/Canadian couple (summer in Massachusetts and winter in Florida) who met in the synagogue 7 years ago. They were really lovely, very gentle and with a wealth of humorous stories. Finally, John and Betty were from Preston in Lancashire and celebrating their golden wedding in September. They were all very supportive of Chris (all had encountered illness, cancer and death somewhere along the line) and it really made every evening a delightful experience.

Our lunch in North Majorca at our favourite Hotel Cala was a delight. They gave us lunch and drinks completely free, and presented Chris with a large and very lovely bouquet of red roses when we left. It was a truly wonderful day.

The Tapas Cookery School in Barcelona was fun, so I am now fully qualified as a Spanish chef! We enjoyed our trip in Corsica, a truly beautiful island to which my few photos do little justice.

Obviously I ate too much – wait until you see the menus before you criticise, I defy you to reject much either – and so left the ship feeling (and looking) like Mr Blobby. The experience of being 'in the posh bit' was also very memorable. Whilst there were 2,100 on the ship (including children), there are just 270 in the Grills. The Grills have their own lounge and own decks, and believe me, there was some serious money aboard (including Jimmy Savile) judging by the dresses and the jewellery. But, it did the job in that Chris didn't have to cope with crowds and risk infection.

Our suite was excellent, plenty big enough to indulge in the regular sleeping that followed eating! The service, as you would expect, was first class but it should be the way Cunard charge tips and gratuities on everything! Jeez, thank goodness the £ has strengthened against the $!

Chris now has to face the next three weeks of treatment, which means more suffering and side-effects after a couple of months of comparative stability. It will come as a bit of a shock to us both, because it has really been the old Chris of late. She has her next set of tests, scans, etc early September so we'll then know whether there has been any change in the tumour. She has been doing so well, maybe 'the miracle' really is happening as she is unrecognisable from the sick little soldier she was earlier in the year. She never needed her wheelchair on board, so although her legs remain painful and tender she is able to walk so much better than before. She is suffering no pain from the tumour, so her morphine intake is minimal.

I would like to start planning our next six months holiday activities but I'm frightened of making too many positive assumptions as we are entering the period that, on average, brings us into the end-game. However, I remain convinced that the positive thinking, the prayers and positive thoughts from all our friends is having a major effect on achieving 'the miracle'.

We are considering a few days in France, 6th – 11th September with my cousin and wife who live in Brittany, but won't make a final decision until after this weekend once we have seen how Chris reacts to this week's treatment.

So, the last two months have been a really positive period for us. Thanks for all your support, prayers, positive thinking, distance healing and all the other 'good vibrations' you have been sending us! Hopefully, next month will maintain Chris's stability and our next update will be just as positive.

Take care and God bless,
Trevor & Chris xxx

Dear Chris & Trev,
Great pictures of you Chris. Weather looks good. Who's the pasty-looking Pom with you though? Needs a bit of sun, I would say.

Cheers,
Laurie (Vogler)

Hey Trev,
Beautiful photos. You both look wonderful. Tell Chris she looks hot and very trendy with the hair. I know quite a few women here who have gone with the shaved head look – fashion statement. Hoping the scan results are good news. How are you coping with everything Trev? Hopefully the cruise holiday is giving you both something to look forward during the rough times you're going through.

Big, big hugs and lots of love as always.
Deb (Hanfeld)

Hi Trev and Chris,
It's good to hear from you and hear some positive news despite all the challenges you have faced during the last few weeks. I admire you both enormously for your courage and strength to fight on and still look forward to your trips and little ventures. I do hope my visit is still okay on Sunday 12th, please let me know if it's too much, and we can rearrange? I am so looking forward to seeing you both, and would be more than happy to cook the lunch, if this helps in any way!

If there is anything I can do, please let me know, as I know and understand the range of emotions you are feeling.

Mike and the children send their love and look forward to hearing from you soon.

Our warmest wishes,
Sian x x x (Ayckbourn)

Hello guys, it was lovely to read your update on your lives and it's great that Chris is able to enjoy the trips you are going on and make the most of the lovely summer we are having. I am sorry the reply is long in coming but we were away then I lost mail then we went away again. We have just come back from Tenby where we surprised my mum who was on holiday. She is nearly 80 so it was nice to spend a few days with her. Please keep me informed how Chris is doing. Do you still go in the pub? Richard is so well, he looks ten years younger. My new toy boy. Well love to you both and we hope to see you both soon in between your holidays and ours.

Love,
Chrissy and Dickie (Probert)

Thanks for the update and the pictures. Chris is certainly looking good. Why did you let that big fat bloke sit with her all the time?

Seriously you are both beaming and the trip sounds fantastic.

Just keep your spirits up.

Many o' them
John and Florence (Oliver)

Hi Trevor,
Yes, I agree its is difficult to see that she is so ill. She does look a picture of health.

We are really pleased that you had such a good time and certainly one which will remain with you always.

We too have been having our own 'bad patch' unfortunately ours does not have a happy note to it.

Sharon's mother took ill in early June and was taken into hospital. The whole family spent 24 hours at her bedside doing the caring alongside the hospital staff. Sharon lived at the hospital for almost 3 weeks leaving home at 8pm, doing the night shift, returning home around 10am the next day. The positive note was that despite having to sign the DNR papers her mom showed them what she was made of and pulled through. Although not able to walk when she was discharged 3 weeks ago, she remained in very positive spirits and we all have said that she was an absolute delight to be with. However, this is where the story ends unfortunately. Having been home only three weeks she died on Tuesday evening after having been rushed into hospital. It was a massive heart attack.

When someone is taken away so quickly it is always difficult that you really did not get the opportunity to say goodbye the way perhaps you would want to.

We are obviously very upset and Sharon is devastated as she has always been devoted to both her parents. She is remaining strong (although tearful when she lets it lapse). Her dad is staying with us at the moment and will be returning home after the funeral next week. She has lots to do as executrix.

Anyway, we sincerely send our wishes that Chris continues to beat the awful thing into a corner.

And as you say sometimes miracles do happen.

Regards,
Tim and Sharon x (Woolridge)

Dear Trevor and Chris,
In just three days, we have heard from you three times, and are very impressed with your communication skills. We are so glad to hear that you and Chris got home safely, and that Chris did so well on our cruise.

We arrived home our time at 8.30 p.m. on Monday, which would have been five hours later for you. The trip was uneventful, but we were very tired of the travel. We are all unpacked, have played bridge with friends and won $2.00. Today we drove about two hours to meet Albie's son,daughter-in-law and grandson at a beautiful museum. This is his California son, and they are taking their son to University today, for a start as a freshman tomorrow.

I must tell you that we watched the video from the ship and you, Chris ,John and Betty are in it. You are arriving at the Captain's cocktail party. It was a good memory for us.

It was wonderful getting to know you on the cruise and we wish for you all that you wish yourselves.

Love,
Miriam and Albie

Wow, what a wonderful update!

So glad to hear that you had such a brilliant trip and that Chris's quality of life is right up there. As it should be! Jimmy Savile eh? Mixing with the stars too....!

My thoughts will be with you over the next few weeks while Chris is undergoing more treatment. Without doubt the miracle is happening already and the fact that she has been in such fighting form is the evidence of it. And long may it continue to be so.

Lots of love to you both,
Sue (Richardson)

Dear Trev & Chris,
I'm glad you had such a great time, both of you, and Chris does look great in the pictures. I'll talk to you soon.

Rowl & Hazel xxx (Charge)

Hi Trev,
Gail and I have both read your update from the office.

We are so encouraged by the progress that has been made, and that the cruise went so well.

Give Chris our love and be assured that you both remain in our thoughts and prayers.

God Bless,
David & Marilyn (Dippie) *[Gail is David's office manager.]*

Dear Trevor,
Wow, what a good idea your deluxe cruise was. Chris looks great and there must be a link between looking good and it doing good too. She radiates happiness. Credit to you for the positive thinking notion that something exciting to do could have such a positive effect.

And you've learnt to cook in Spanish too!

I shall be thinking of you both over this fortnight as I can imagine how the chemo side-effect is a constant worry. Chris is amazing – she has and is being a daily reminder of the value of positive thought. Please give her a big hug and a kiss from me. As for you, well you are certainly looking the part – wealthy and in rude health! Anyway, one takes it as read that taking a cruise will always add a couple of pounds!

I am keeping everything crossed for the next 2 weeks after which I really hope you can take Chris off to France. I'm sure you will too.

My best wishes to you both. Yours aye,
Tony (Wightman)

This is so well written and so very touching Trevor, fingers crossed tightly for the next phase.

Love from us all,
Tim (Kidson)

Hi Trev,
It was great to get your latest news and to see Chris looking happy on your holiday – it sounds like it did you both the world of good. I hope that the treatment this week etc. is not hitting her too hard. I was hoping to call up and see you a couple of weeks ago, but we unfortunately had a horrible little criminal in custody who also had swine flu and we were advised not to go and visit anyone who may be vulnerable in case we were to have caught it and passed it on without realising, so I have kept away from most people for the past few weeks. Thankfully I haven't (touch wood) so far come out with it. It is sad really because I haven't been able to go and see my Nan either (she is now 99 years old - unfortunately has senile dementia so she wouldn't know that I haven't been to see her but I still miss her as I usually try and go every couple of weeks - she is in the care home at Chipping Norton).

Well I am off to Andrea's wedding on Friday - she is tying the knot with Martin (the guy she met from Paintbox where she went to work). I am so looking forward to it - can't remember the last time I went to a wedding. Anyway I will take lots of photos and will send you one of the blushing bride.

Give my love to Chris - and a big (but very gentle) hug, tell her I am thinking of her and praying for you both.

God bless.
Chrisy xx (Cross)

Hi to you both, I was so pleased to hear you have had such a wonderful time on your cruise. I told you the food was good didn't I? I took two evening dresses on our cruise, for the formal evenings, but had to wear the same one twice as by the time it got to the second formal evening I couldn't fit comfortably into the other dress. Hooray for shift dresses is all I can say! It was so lovely to see you looking so healthy, Christine, long may you stay that way. I know the chemo will knock you sideways for a while but hopefully you will bounce back again soon.

We are off to Bulgaria on the 24th which should be great fun.

Looking forward to hearing from you again soon,

all our love,
Lesley, Dean and boys xxxxxxx (Carpenter)

Hi Trevor,
What a great letter. I am so pleased that Chris is looking so well and that the cruise gave you everything that you were looking for and so much deserve. As you say positive thinking is the best medicine of all and our thoughts are with you.

Take care. A catch up would be good.

All the best
John (Frost)

Hi Trevor,
How lovely to hear from you and get such a fantastic report on how well the cruise went for you and Chris. The photos are truly wonderful and show Chris so happy and contented; most of this is due I guess to the holiday and the luxury, but she does also have a lovely and caring nurse in you Trev.

Best of luck for the next stage of treatment, as I know this won't be easy for both of you, especially Chris, so I do wish you all the strength and hope that you will get through this next hurdle and then look forward to your next little jaunt.

Sadly for us my sister is really sick and not a picture of happiness like Chris. She is deteriorating very quickly now since her lung has collapsed and it does not help with the good lung having a great big blood clot. She is unable to care for herself and is pretty much in bed everyday. Despite all our prayers and rota of care she has no respite. June has her review on Monday, and right now we are not overly optimistic about the doctor's report. I am leaving for Wales tomorrow for a few days, to take over from my niece who is struggling to keep it all together.

Trev, I wish you and Chris all the love in the world and we will still continue to hold you in our prayers. It's so lovely to hear some positive news.

All my love,
Sian x x x x (Ayckbourn)

Hello Trevor and Chris,
What fantastic news I am so delighted that Chris is so well and enjoyed the holiday which gives her good memories to cling onto for the chemo, which I know is not much fun. I will be thinking of her during that time. Here's to another 6 months.

Love Clare (Farrands)

Hi you guys, how lovely to hear from you and we do like to be kept up to date with Chris's progress. You both are in our thoughts and prayers. Chris looks great in the pictures and you both look as though you are loving the cruise and yes how the other half live! But it is good that everything seems to be at a hold and god willing Chris will enjoy all that you are experiencing together. I will keep Chris in my prayers. Richard is very well but has a bit of hand and feet swelling so he had a blood test on Friday. We are still travelling in the motor home but Jackie is home for a month now so we are home with her. I am slowly going out of my mind as I miss work so much but i hope Dickie will let us do relieving from October till the spring then we can travel again in the motor home. Housework, gardening and the dogs are just not enough for me. I need to have a challenge in my life. Dickie can't understand me and says anyone would give everything to be doing what we are doing but it isn't enough for me. I will end up in the nut house if I don't get back to work.

Well once again thanks for keeping us informed and God bless you both.
Chrissy and Dickie (Probert)

Chris poolside for lunch at our favourite hotel in the whole world - Hotel Cala,
Cala San Vicenc, Majorca (July 2009)

The Ballad Of Lucy Jordan

~ Marianne Faithfull ~

Kerdruc, Brittany, - it is almost impossible to believe Chris was so il! (September 2009)

~ The Ballad of Lucy Jordan ~

August was a month where we just eased a little, took a deep breath and realised that we were living a miracle. The four months we had been quoted had turned into eight months, so our view was that every day was a bonus. The miracle all our friends were praying for with us was actually taking place. We never truly believed that a miracle was going to be a cure, and this month gave us time to begin to understand where we were at!

It was also the month I sought support on the forum of Pancreatic Cancer UK. I felt I needed to communicate with others in the same situation, despite the great support we were receiving from our family and friends. The support I received from fellow carers of pancreatic cancer patients was truly fantastic. We all supported each other in the best way we could with information, little stories of hope and reading updates on developments in the treatment desperately seeking anything that could be used with our loved ones. It is a place where I could express my inner thoughts to individuals who understood my worries and the emotions that I was going through.

Cancer of the pancreas is a vicious disease, unforgiving and aggressive. It is under resourced and under researched in the UK. As a result, its mortality rate is the worst of any cancer. The nation needs to wake-up and smell the coffee regarding preventive medicine for pancreatic cancer.

Chris had a lumbar spine x-ray mid-month as part of the ongoing checks on her bones. The doctors seemed more concerned about this than we were. Chris wasn't suffering at all with aches, etc. so maybe we were being just a bit too relaxed. Chris dealt with her chemotherapy in her usual unflappable way and we began our build-up to our short visit to Brittany.

Once again our insurance was done with MIA Online, who are a terrific company. They dealt with Chris's travel Insurance every time we travelled. They did so efficiently and very cost effectively.

We sailed over to Roscoff on 7th September. We enjoyed a typically good Brittany Ferry dinner, then retired to our cabin. The crossing was uneventful and Chris had no sickness issues. What we had tried to do every time with our holidays was to arrange them after Chris had had a week's break from chemotherapy. This gave her a chance to have recovered from the side-effects and be at her best for the travelling and holiday.

Our days in Brittany were wonderful. Chris was as good as she had been on our cruise. If you didn't know she was a bit thinner than normal you would never know she was so ill. She walked, suffered no serious tiredness and the weather (as usual for Chris during any of the year's holidays) was blue skies and sunshine! Maybe it does shine on the righteous! Derrick and Yvonne were so kind, Pistache the cat even condescended to come to us for a stroke and so, once again, this desperately sad year was enlivened by a week of happiness.

Chris and I had been in love with France for over 20 years. Our wine buying trips have become legendary with our friends, indeed we have travelled with friends several times on those trips. It was important to me that Chris visit France before she was too ill. It gave her a chance to say her own farewell to the country, and discover a new part of the country as well. She may not have 'driven through Paris with the wind in her hair' as the chapter song says, but in reality she had done it many times in a different way.

We returned to another chemotherapy treatment and a consultant's meeting with Dr Mehra. Generally he was happy with Chris, but concerned at possible spread into her bones. We were less worried than him, while in truth Chris had no worry at all. 'He's wrong', she said, 'I'm fine'. Nothing changes.

Chemotherapy	August 21st
	August 28th
September 18th	Consultant: Oncologist
August 17th	Lumbar spine x-ray -

Update No 7 – 19th September 2009

Hi,

It is 6 weeks since our latest update, and 8 months since Chris was diagnosed and given approx 4 months survival! So, we've doubled the original prognosis which is a really great result and better than any of us could hope for.

Today we have had a meeting with her oncologist, and it's fair to say we have had mixed results. The bad news is that there is the likelihood that there has been spread into Chris's lower back (in a vertebra) and also in her upper right femur. To quote the oncologist, 'there is a change of texture and density'. He has told us to closely monitor any pain in those areas and report immediately any increase (currently Chris has none, she has had one day of back-pain about 2 weeks ago).

The other 'bad' news was that Chris's cancer count (Tumour Marker CA19-9) which is provided by blood test, has increased up to 803 from below 100. However, he thought this was possibly due to Chris having had no treatment for three weeks (until today) and he will monitor closely after this next 3-week cycle of treatment. She will also be due another CT scan after this cycle.

This must all be counter-balanced by the fact that Chris is currently in fine form (always, please, consider this to be relative - she is not strong enough to do much in the way of household chores, potter in the garden or walk more than about 100 metres) and compared to many people is able to live a pretty 'normal' life.

Since our last update, our latest little jaunt was to visit my cousin Derrick and his wife Yvonne in Brittany for five days w/c 7th Sept. We had a wonderful time, the weather was splendidly warm, the skies blue and the hospitality outstanding. We visited several places around Tregunc, including Quimper, Loncronan, Port Aven and Port Maniche and enjoyed some lovely meals from Yvonne plus a night out at a local restaurant. Chris handled the ferry journeys Plymouth – Roscoff really well (we had a cabin both ways) and so yet another successful break! 3 Pictures attached.

Chris coped with her 3 treatments in August pretty well, her legs only marginally worsening and not reducing her to the wheelchair. She became increasingly tired over the weeks, but nothing that she couldn't handle.

We are currently planning a trip to Ireland in October to visit our friends Tony and Ann Killoran (old pals from my BASF days when Tony was MD of Golden Discs), subject to Chris being comfortable with another ferry crossing. Then, in November (25th) we're off to try P&O for a 13 day cruise to the Canaries & Madeira in order to give Chris some winter sunshine before Christmas. Nothing as grand as our Grills experience on Queen Victoria but we're interested to compare!

As always, a big thank you to all our friends who are providing such support and guidance as we travel this awful journey together. It is you who are making the 'the miracle' take place and helping inspire Chris every month. Please keep the emails etc coming, and the prayers and positive thinking remain central to sustaining the battle.

Finally, visitors are crucial in helping Chris keep on fighting. We would love to see you, but please call and then we can plan in the diary to ensure that Chris is not over-taxed.

God bless and take care
Trev & Chris
xxx

Hi Trev,
Glad to hear you and Chris are in such positive frame of mind and have so many fun things planned. Keep up the good work.

I am not doing too well at the moment - I am in hospital right now - I had a stroke on Wednesday - I am feeling better now but confined to bed in ICU - but at least - can think straight now - You just never know what is round the corner!!

Take care
Love Shirl (Hunter)

Trevor & Chris,
We so appreciate your emails keeping us in touch with Chris's fight for survival and apologise for not keeping in touch more often. She must have so much spirit and you, Trevor, must give her the strength she needs to carry on. Your holidays must help her to keep going. With the cancer spreading to the lower back and upper right femur I can't believe she is not in more pain but I hope the pain stays away.

I go into the fund raising office of Macmillan Cancer Support once a week to help out in the office, Monday 21st may be the last for a week or two but they will soon phone me to help with something else.

We think of you both constantly and hope and pray we will have many more emails from you with good rather than bad news of Chris's progress. In between all your holidays we will try and get to see you.

God bless,
Pat & Brian (Bourne)

Trevor
Thank you for updating us on Chris - We think about her all the time. We go to Spain as you know from tomorrow but will keep in touch. We are back on the 8th October so we will speak then.

The very best wishes to you both but special HUGS & KISSES to Chris.
Michael & Sue (Parker)

Hello Trevor,

Thank you for the update e-mail. Chris looks really blooming (& her old self) in these photos. It's really had to believe that she is very ill!

Carol & I think & talk a lot about you two, & you both are never very far from our thoughts & prayers. Let me know if you have a spare weekend date that's free in November??

Take care of yourselves. Best wishes,
Carol & Gary (Milner)

Hi What lovely news that you and Chris are remaining positive. Hil lived on that positivity for 4 years, much longer than predicted. So miracles do happen. Our love prayers and thoughts for you.

Regards
Clare. (Farrands)

Hello Trevor,

What an inspiration Chris is to everyone reading your updates, especially to those of us who have ever complained of a 'headache' or 'cold'. I am sure your little breaks are helping and certainly giving Chris something positive to look forward to.

Sean and I have just had a few days off together. Normally at this time of year we would have gone off to sunnier shores but this year we have stayed at home with a list of things to do. One of my tasks was to sort the garden out and catch up on all the jobs I never have time to get around to doing. Although we love to go off abroad I can honestly say we did enjoy our time at home (nicknamed staycation)

I hope you and Chris enjoy your trip to Ireland and look forward to reading your next update.

Take care. Love and best wishes to you both.
Liz & Sean (Forde) xx

Hi both,thanks for the photos I think Chris is looking pretty well considering, and you obviously had lovely weather. I pray that the pain in her back and legs stays away,and that you can do the next 2 planned hols.

Love to you both,
Rosemary and Jim (Allan)

Hello Trevor,

Thank you for all your recent reports on Chris's condition and progress, together with photographs of all your trips/breaks. They must have done you both a lot of good. Chris looks so well, considering. I will continue to pray for her, that's all we can do.

I have just had some sad news from a friend of mine I used to work with, Shirley Venman at BASF Haddon House. I don't think that you would have met her. She moved to Stratford a few years ago as her husband had his workplace there. About a year ago, he started feeling unwell and was diagnosed with cancer of the colon; was given treatment a year ago, but with little hope for cure. I got the news that he passed away last Sunday - he was only 53.

Best wishes to you and Christine,
Ulla (Pschierer)

Hi Chum,

Denise and I have just returned from a fortnight in the Lot Valley in France, so I'm a bit behind with correspondence.

It's great to hear how strong positivity can achieve so much. From the snaps, Chris looks in good shape and one really would not even consider she has so much to deal with. She is an inspiration to others. As ever, you're keeping things moving along with a trip to Ireland followed by another cruise, to the Canaries and Madeira this time! I appreciate how much time, effort, imagination and money not least, all this involves on your part. But it is a winning strategy.

Please give Chris our love and best wishes, and the same goes for you too.

Yours aye,
Tony (Wightman)

Hi Chris & Trev,

Great to talk to you this morning. You sounded great Chris. Go girl. Just came across these photos from an Arrawarra trip.

Love,
Deb (Hanfeld)

Dear Trevor and Chris,

Thank you for your update always lovely to hear from you. Just a quick note to say hope things are still going well? And your October trip to Ireland goes well. It makes a difference when you're surrounded by love and support, well done Chris! And you Trevor.

Love and best wishes,
Allison, Bill and Jean McNally x

Viewing the gift shops in Locranon, Brittany (September 2009)

WEDDING SONG

~Bob Dylan ~

Rowl and Hazel's Wedding: Chris, Marie, Audrey, Dave and Rob. Our longest standing friends - we go back nearly fifty years! (September 2009)

~ Wedding Song ~

Our main event at the end of this month, after our trip to France, was being able to attend Rowl and Hazel's wedding at Belper, Derbyshire on September 26th. When we put this date in our diary, I think in truth we both wondered whether Chris would be able to attend. In fact, Chris was once again at her radiant best.

She was truly amazing in her ability to overcome (and ignore) her pain, her illness and everything connected with it. She continued to refuse early nights, maintaining that a gin and tonic or a red wine was far better for her than all the drugs. It seems odd to say that she was 'radiant' but she truly was. I have the photos to prove it. Her indomitable will and spirit became a beacon to all our friends and especially to me. Alone, late at night, there were many occasions when I cried uncontrollably but always, when I saw Chris the next day, I was picked up and reminded that Chris wasn't crying for herself so I really shouldn't be crying for myself.

We drove up on the Friday. One of the things we established very early in Chris's illness was that she simply could not rush in the mornings. We had to take it very steady, with no stress or pressure to meet deadline times. Chris then suffered no reaction. Therefore, we travelled everywhere a day in advance so that there were no early starts and no rushing.

The wedding day was lovely, old friends gathered together. Chris just like her old, fit self. These long-standing friends have been the cornerstone of all the friends who have been giving us so much. There are no words to thank Dave and Marie for their dependable love and support. Rowl and Hazel, Rob and Aud have all been such friends through the years but now, in our darkest moments, they have come to mean even more. I only hope they realise how they have helped us this year.

Night at the pub with the lads, Chris drinking G&Ts pre-wedding, champagne, etc. We had a great couple of days.

Bearing in mind Chris had received some chemotherapy on the Friday, she was really well over this weekend. We left the hotel and called at Tony and Sue (Chris's younger brother) for lunch. I think Tony has had a real problem dealing with Chris's illness. As the youngest I guess he thinks of his older brothers and sisters as indestructible, so when a big sister was told she only had three months to live his faith was suddenly shattered.

One of the things we have learnt is that individuals deal with imminent death (and particularly cancer) in very individual ways. Some friends admitted to me they couldn't handle the thought of seeing Chris suffer, go downhill, lose weight, etc so they didn't come and visit her. We understood this but felt it was a big loss to both sides. Visitors kept Chris going, gave her reasons to fight on. The visitors who came were all, without exception, inspired in their lives by Chris and her attitude.

At least once a month we lunched with Barry and Carol, friends who had always brought us sunshine and laughter. Chris loved our times with them, they treated her just as they always had without fussing over her illness. Chris liked that, she was not after tea and sympathy but just a normal life. We laughed at many things together over the year, often with a black humour about death. They were another couple of friends who became ever more important in our lives during the year.

Chemotherapy:	September 25th October 2nd October 16th
October 12th	CT Scan:
October 16th	Consultant: Oncologist –

Update No 8 – 16th October 2009

Hi,

Well, another month has passed and I am pleased to report that Chris is stable. She had her first CT scans since April last Monday, and we saw her oncologist today to be told that there has been no change in her condition. The tumour has not grown, and there does not appear to be any significant spread. He is uncertain whether the minor changes that showed up in the bone X-rays last month actually are a cancer spread because Chris is suffering absolutely no pain in those areas. Crucially, there is no sign of spread into her lungs, or into her lymphs, so we came away greatly encouraged.

Typically, Chris remarked that 'Well, I will be seeing Christmas then' which was another example of her unflappable way of dealing with this.

As you will remember, the original survival prognosis was 4 months. The doctors issued the 'less than 6 months' note for benefit claims. But surviving until today means that Chris has today reached 9 months since she collapsed with the pain – and 9 months is the average survival time! So, the brilliant thing is that we are now into 'bonus days'. Chris has achieved this because she has taken such a positive approach (I'll be alright!) but critically because of your help/support and the help and prayers of all our friends and family around the world. These have helped so much, knowing that so many people are thinking of us and sending positive vibrations! So – take a bow and accept our thanks.

Our next target is to be one of the 10% of pancreatic cancer sufferers who survive 12 months (that's January 15th 2010).

Not every sufferer receives Chris's level of support, and there is also insufficient research being done (sadly it is not a 'sexy' cancer for research or donations). I receive support from Pancreatic Cancer UK via their website, and I try to help other sufferers and carers via their discussion forums. In case you would like to help rectify these situations, I have attached Order Forms from Pancreatic Cancer UK for their Christmas Cards and a few other items.

Unfortunately we never made it to Dublin this month because of the dates clashing with the scan and today's appointment, but the results have helped to partly compensate for missing out on the trip. Tony and Ann sent a truly magnificent bouquet of flowers to Chris after we pulled out of the trip, so I can only repeat our thanks to them both.

Fortunately Chris's problems with her legs are also stable, which means that we are able to meet friends for lunch and have little trips out in the day. We made it our friends Rowl and Hazel's wedding (staying for the weekend in the Peak District), and we're off to stay with Rob and Pippa this weekend. Of course, our next great adventure is 25th November when we set off for 13 nights to the Canary Islands (and Madeira) with P&O on Arcadia. After today, we are both more confident that Chris will be ok.

Her chemotherapy has been reduced to 60% of the initial levels she received in February which also means that she suffers less side-effects. She began her next 3 treatments today (after 2 weeks off), so we are hoping she copes with it ok.

We have received a dose of reality in the last week as well. Our dear friend Sian lost her sister to lung cancer last weekend after a fairly short (in cancer terms) period of illness, whilst on Wednesday I attended the funeral of Susie Sharman. Susie and Chris had been fighting in parallel this year (although Susie was first diagnosed with breast cancer a couple of years ago) and Susie and Kim were on a cruise only 3 weeks ago. So, Chris and I are acutely aware this thing can bite you back very hard and very quickly. Hence, our policy of living every day and planning the good things of life.

I'll report again before we embark in November. Please remember, visitors are always welcome – they are a key part in the 'positive attitude' strategy plus it means Chris doesn't get even more bored with me than she already is! - and all emails, letters etc are received with thanks and appreciation. If you would like to phone to speak to Chris, please ring after 11.00 in the morning – she never did mornings anyway, and does them even less now!

Take care and God Bless,
Trevor & Chris

xxx

Trev,
It is so good to hear such positive news on Chris, she is fighting for every minute. I am so proud to know her.

I had a little scare myself last month – I had a stroke ! Forgive me if I have told you this already – I forget a lot these days – I am going to start and write a book before I forget it all!!

I am better now – I have lost 10lbs and am walking 2miles every day and trying to cut down the stress. I am thinking It could almost be time to retire! Can I really be that old?
Shirl (Hunter)

Hi Trev and Chris,
Great news! It all sounds quite positive. I hope you enjoy the cruise as much as you did the previous one.

Let's Skype again (like we did last summer).
Geoff Owens

Hi Trevor, Hi Chris,
Thanks a million for the latest report which is most encouraging. Chris certainly has

some guts. Sorry you had to cancel your Dublin trip - perhaps in the New Year eh? We have decided to visit our daughter in America for Christmas, and will be over there from 14th – 28th December. Do give Chris all our love and best wishes - you are still in our thoughts and prayers every single day.

Love and respect,
John.(Edmundson)

Trevor,
This is so encouraging to hear and we continue to pray and hope for you guys. I hope you are able to get away together soon again.

God bless to you both,
Dave (Tubby)

Hi Trevor,
Thanks for keeping us in the picture; you're both always in our thoughts. The power of goodwill, positivity and love are far beyond anything medical science has dreamed or dares to admit.

I hope we'll get the chance to meet up again before too long.

Take care,
Jem (Shaw)

19th October 2009 – My thoughts Written late at night

Late at night the music played
Harmonicas, guitars and drums
Voices of our favourites
Tunes that we hummed

Looking in eyes
Touching each other
Where were we at these moments
That meant so much

Now you're going away
Sometime, sooner than we thought
Leaving me to remember
And you to float along

It's thanks for the memories
Thanks for the years
Thanks for the beauty
Thanks for the tears
Thanks for the teaching, of our souls
But most it's thanks
For it all

All those years, the love that you gave
The power you passed, the strength that you laid
I never knew how much it all meant
Until they told us that we were being cut short
I can't tell anyone what you meant
You passed through my world
But you are my world, Without you there is no world
I may not make it

Hi Trevor & Chris,

Thanks for the emails, reading your reports makes me proud to have you as my family, such strength and compassion and a healthy dose of humour. After seeing all your brilliant pictures of your holidays (in the sun!!) I thought I would send you some pictures of our last camping holiday (seeing the sun for the first time in 5 days was a cause to take pictures!!) It reminds me of all the camping trips when we were kids. Happy days!!

Hope you enjoy all your holidays and look forward to seeing you at the Christmas dinner!!
Martin, Leigh, Isabelle, Charlotte (Loynes)

Good report, Trev,

Glad that things are not getting worse, tho' attending the funerals cannot have been easy.

Take care and love to you both,
John (Caruth)

Keep up the fight.
Clive (Fowler)

Thank you Trevor,

We read your reports with great enthusiasm and our thoughts, love and support are with Chris, you and your family.

My Mum, bless her, passed away just three weeks ago after a very short illness and I am finding it difficult to get my head round her not being with us.

Please give Chris a big hug from both of us,
Jeff & Tina xx (Hull)

Dear Trevor,

Many thanks for your email and we were very pleased that the news on Chris is good and it is hoped that the condition will continue to improve. Her attitude towards this is obviously the right one. It's good that you have a holiday to look forward to and the sunshine will help too.

With our best wishes and our thoughts will be with you.
Jim & Joyce (Williams)

Hi Chris & Trev,

You know we pray for you every night, and continue to believe God's love and presence will be with you both. It's good to receive such encouraging news.

My own sister (also Chris) developed Parkinson's and Distonia 3 years ago (aged 58 at the time) and now has to use a wheelchair for shopping, so both Chris's are constantly in our thoughts. It's good that you continue to fill your lives with positive thoughts and actions.

Take care, and God bless you both.
David & Marilyn (Dippie)

Dear Christine,

I know this sounds a bit silly, but I was sat in the bath a few weeks ago and I was thinking about you. While thinking of you I had a really beautiful picture of butterflies. One of my friends makes cards, so I asked her if she could make me a card with butterflies on and, as you can see, this (card) is the result.

I do hope you like it. This is just a little note to let you know that I am thinking about you and the family and to tell you that Jane and I are praying for you and send you lots of love and hugs.

Lots of love from Val (Facey) xxx

To Christine,

Just to let you know you're in our thoughts.

Lots of love,

Tara, Anthony & Lily-Mae xxx

Email sent from Chris

For all the ladies,

From Chris xxx

Be the kind of woman that when your feet hit the floor each morning the devil says 'Oh Crap, She's up!'

Sister

Life is too short to wake up with regrets

so love the people who treat you right

Love the ones who don't just because you can

Believe everything happens for a reason

If you get a second chance, grab it with both hands

If it changes your life, let it

Kiss slowly

Forgive quickly

God never said life would be easy

He just promised it would be worth it.

Hello Chris,

Thank you so much for the email it is very moving.

I have always had the utmost admiration for you ever since we met on Queen Vic. and am so moved by your fighting ability. I send you all my love, and best wishes for a continued improvement in your health. John reminds me that you are off on another cruise shortly - have a great time I just wish we were going as well. We are going to visit our daughter in America for Christmas, so we are looking forward to that immensely.

Have a great cruise, continue to improve, and my love to you

Betty. xxx (Edmundson)

Dearest Chris,

I loved this - it's such a great way to start the day.

Thanking you so much for sending.

Loving and healthy thoughts from me to you everyday. Be well, stay well.
Love Debbie (Murrish)

I hope you are both well xxx Suzanne (Smith)

Trevor,
It is great to receive these updates as it really keeps the progress fresh and relevant in one's mind. And thanks too for keeping me on the list.

Chris never ceases to amaze – her spirit is indomitable, yet I'm sure the effort must seem humongous. I know how the chemo can knock her back a bit, so I'm keeping my fingers crossed she deals with this period well.

Good luck with the cruise, and I do hope you will both find it an enjoyable next adventure (watch out crossing the Bay of Biscay though!) – I've done it but not in anything the size of Arcadia of course. We were sailing a 40ft yacht!

Love and best wishes from both of us to both of you,

Yours aye,
Tony (Wightman)

Dear Trevor,
As always – Carol and I really like receiving your periodical update e-mails, and we very much appreciate being able to follow Chris and your progress over the weeks and months. From my side you guys make me feel very privileged and actually I have absolutely nothing to complain about (although, being just human – I of course do complain!)

Your e-mails help provide me with a kind of reference point. I mean, I know that you'll understand (can remember) the continuous pressure of working in a corporate environment. I feel that I have been working flat out for most of this year, with only a few weeks holiday as a break from the pace. Now we're into the 4th quarter – the busy period – when things really get going.

As an example of what I am talking about - I'm writing this e-mail to you from a US Airways flight to Charlotte NC during Sunday AM (when the rest of the sensible world is sleeping in). We have a world-wide 2010 budget planning meeting in Charlotte and in advance of this session we have booked a world-wide product planning event (actually it was my idea to have the two meetings – one after the other), but still I am away for yet another full working week, and expect to be back home in Blighty sometime during mid morning next Saturday.

You might be surprised to learn that despite rumours from some parts of the company – we're doing rather well here in Verbatim EUMEA (well everything is relative – looks likely that we will hit our US$ EBT/ EFO numbers – which given the general economic environment is not too bad, and believe me looks outstanding compared to my opposite number colleagues for Asia Pacific or indeed the Americas regions.

Anyway, enough of my wittering on. Please pass on our regards, thoughts and prayers to Chris. I already mentioned (in a previous e-mail) that Carol has to undergo some surgery to her shoulder at the end of this month – so my idea is that we will contact you when she is the recovery phase - and fix up a date to meet up.

OK, all for now – I have to get back to some work – need to make this trip pay.

Take care of yourselves. We are always thinking of you.

Best wishes,
Gary & Carol (Milner)

Hi Trev,
Thanks for the update. It is absolutely brilliant news. What an inspiration you both are! I'm quite sure you will have a wonderful time on the cruise and can look forward to a wonderful Christmas.

Thinking of you always. Love & hugs,
Deb (Hanfeld)

Many thanks for e-mail, always thinking of you both, obviously Chris (I'm going to get Tango'd today) remember Chris? I really cannot forget that.

Love to both,
Philip and Val (Burton)

Hello guys,
Just picked up your e mail - we have been on holiday since September 20th so have not checked the PC, It is great news and it is your love and devotion which has given Christine such hope and God willing will see you both through. It is so good to hear your news we have just come back from Jamaica where we spent our 40th anniversary.

I have some news. I am going to run a pub for a little while for my Jo. It is the Swan at Upton near Bromsgrove so we won't be too far away. I am a bit scared as I start on Monday in Wales for training but I only want to do it for 18 months or so. It needs a great deal of cleaning up and staff training so I will have my hands full for a little while. Dickie and I will ring and come and see you as soon as we take over. Enjoy your cruise and we will see you soon.

Always in our prayers,
Dickie and Chrissy (Probert)

Hi Trevor,
These are really great pictures. Thanks for sending.

So glad to hear that Chris is doing well and that plans for your trip in November are going forward.

Please tell Chris I think of her often and pray for her well being.

Please keep in touch and have a wonderful time on your November trip. We will want to hear all about it as they always sound like such a great time.

Always remember (and I know you do) that miracles do happen. After all, the word had to come from somewhere - right?

Take care - hope to hear from you both soon.
Love, Debbie and Gary (Murrish)

Dear Chris and Trevor,
It was a joy for us to spend a few hours with you, we are full of admiration at the way in which you're dealing with such a difficult situation.

I've just been re-reading George Carlin's piece on Ageing which you kindly sent. It's got a really good feel and his advice could easily have been written by you two.

Val and I send our love and every good wish.
Peter (Halman)

Hi Peter & Val,
Thank you for your note and your kind words. It was wonderful to see you both
again – after all, it's just been too long – and we were delighted to find you both
keeping so well. Chris really enjoyed the day, and we had a splendid evening and
Sunday with Robert and family so it was a very special weekend for us. When we

tell people that 'our first boss' from all those years ago has been to see us, people simply look at us in amazement and it really does mean a great deal to have become friends over all these years.

I will keep you posted, and thank you once again for coming to see us.

God bless,
Trevor & Chris
xxx

Hello Trevor,
Very well done once more – almost too painful for me to read – but then Chris report no 8 was very tough too. So I don't really know what to say Trevor because this is all outside my remit, my comfort zone, call it what you will.

But I am in there somewhere, thinking of Chris, thinking of you and thinking of all the people that could be in there somewhere too.

All the very best for now,
Tim (Kidson)

The Story Behind 'I Wish You Enough'

'That's a wish that has been handed down from other generations. My parents used to say it to everyone...'

He paused a moment and looked up as if trying to remember it in detail, and he smiled even more. 'When we said, "I wish you enough", we were wanting the other person to have a life filled with just enough good things to sustain them.'

Then turning toward me, he shared the following as if he were reciting it from memory.

I wish you enough sun to keep your attitude bright no matter how grey the day may appear.
I wish you enough rain to appreciate the sun even more.
I wish you enough happiness to keep your spirit alive and everlasting.
I wish you enough pain so that even the smallest of joys in life may appear bigger.
I wish you enough gain to satisfy your wanting.
I wish you enough loss to appreciate all that you possess.
I wish you enough hellos to get you through the final good-bye.

He then began to cry and walked away.

They say it takes a minute to find a special person, an hour to appreciate them, a day to love them; but then an entire life to forget them.

Take time to live...

To all my friends and loved ones, I wish you enough !

Thanks for that Trevor, it makes moving reading. Still thinking about you both daily-hope Chris is still better side out.

Love,
John & Betty. (Edmundson)

Trevor,
Thank you for this, one to make you smile and make you cry.

God Bless,
Liz (Spencer)

Dear Trevor,
So sorry as I am getting back to you late on this.

This is just beautiful - I loved it.

I will send it on -Thank you so much for sending . . .

Please remember, to both you and Chris, 'I Wish You Enough'

Love,
Debbie (Murrish)

Good to hear from you. Yes please add us to the list of people you send your updates to so we know that you and Chris know we are thinking of you.

Chris is clearly a remarkable person and we are full of admiration for her and you.

Best wishes,
Steve (Goodman) & Tony (Ericson)

Hello Chris, and Hello Trevor
Many thanks for your latest update on Chris' health. It is pleasing to know that she is still enjoying life as much as her condition will allow and that you had a good time

in France - hope you have another great visit to Ireland - a touch of the 'Black Stuff' never did an invalid any harm My Grandmother had a glass of Guinness every day for as long as I could remember - she hated the taste but it did her such a lot of good!

Our Golden Wedding finally arrived - last Saturday the 12th - and we had 33 friends and family out for dinner at a local pub which treats us very well as we are regular visitors there. Wednesday saw my 72nd birthday, so we pigged out again at a different local hostelry (just the two of us plus Sal and her husband).

Tell Chris we think of her every day and admire her plucky attitude - I hope I can be that brave when my time comes, she is a marvel. You are both in our daily prayers.

Love and respect,
John (Edmundson)

Hi Trevor,
Many thanks for this. Yes I think it is good for you to be able to get out a bit. Maybe the thing to do is choose carefully the events you attend and those you miss. Trouble is that where you are known, people expect a 'performance' and for one reason or another you may prefer to keep yourself to yourself.

Chris sounds like an amazing lady. But as for the team, well when I get abuse from my Liverpool, Arsenal, Chelsea colleagues and associates I just say that after having won everything for twelve years, we are rebuilding. Isn't that a reasonable thing to be allowed to do? Plus it gives their rabble a chance to win something.

Apparently you can't even get a cup of tea at Anfield these days. All the mugs are on the field and all the cups are at Old Trafford. Tee hee.

As for the great Bob Dylan, anything you have is wonderful therapy for me as I drive around the country. We have loads of work!

They were playing Blonde on Blonde in our local last night.

Best for now to you and Chris.
Tim (Kidson)

Hi to you both,
We are so glad to hear such positive news. It just shows that not getting stressed and just taking each day as it comes has had a major effect on how the cancer has

progressed. We can all learn a lot from you both on how to make the most of life and live it to the full even in times of crisis.

Dean's sciatic problem is still on going. He is now waiting for an appointment for an epidural steroid injection which hopefully will sort things out. All this means Afghanistan is off for him at the moment which I'm pleased about. He is really gutted though.

The boys are both well. James spends most of his free time in a horizontal position, but as he becomes a teenager next week I don't suppose I should expect anything else!! Lewis on the other hand never stops moving! We all got soaked to the skin watching him play rugby this morning, but we soon dried once home.

I hope Robert, Pippa and the children are well and that you had a good weekend with them. We are looking forward to hearing about the cruise. When you get back, don't forget to send us some photos. We hope you have a fantastic time and that you are well enough to really enjoy it Christine.

All our love and positive thoughts as always.
Lesley, Dean, James and Lewis xxxxxxxxxx (Carpenter)

Hi Trevor and Chris,
I am sorry I didn't get to visit you the other week. I spent a week in hospital with abdo pain which has been resolved; they also found on the scan that I have a small lesion on my pancreas which has been biopsied in Birmingham this week! The consultant assured me it is a benign cyst but I will now need yearly MRI scans to keep an eye on it.

Hopefully I will get to see you in the next few weeks and I send you lots of love.
Lindsay (Townend)
x

Hi Trevor,
Thanks for the call yesterday. How are things today? My thoughts are with you both.

Take care,
Janet (Peacock)

HAVE I TOLD YOU LATELY THAT I LOVE YOU

~ Van Morrison ~

~ Have I Told You Lately That I Love You ~

Chris's arms began to deteriorate in this period, culminating in real problems in November. Little did we know that we were actually seeing the beginning of the end of Chris's miracle even though we had one more good holiday left together.

She began to complain of pain in her arms similar to the leg pain suffered back in June. Then, stopping chemotherapy did the trick. This time it didn't. Her chemotherapy on October 30th proved to be the last one she ever received.

The registrar was unable to help at our meeting, although she arranged for both a CT Scan and Ultrasound (to check for blood clots) as a matter of urgency.

These were difficult days with Chris being in real pain with her arms, for perhaps the 1st time in 5 months. Maybe we had grown complacent, underestimating the destructiveness of the cancer. Maybe the miracle she was living had made us too relaxed, too much assuming things would be 'alright'.

Whatever the reasons, these became shocking and dispiriting days. We truly thought we were going to have to cancel our cruise we had booked for later in the month.

Chemotherapy   *October 23rd*
          October 30th

November 5th   *Consultant: Oncologist Registrar –*

Update No 9 – 6th November 2009

Hi,

Chris has continued to be stable until this week, but this has been our worst since June. Chris appears to have had another bad reaction to her treatment (as she did in June) resulting in swollen legs and arms with extreme pain in them and too tender to touch. This is allied to the usual side-effects of tiredness, occasional bouts of sickness, loss of appetite etc.

The medicos basically have no real idea what is causing the reaction (if that is what it is). She underwent an ultrasound on Thursday to check for blood clots, which proved negative, and will have another CT Scan asap. They have no remedy to rectify the situation which means we have had to increase her pain-killers (which includes morphine), which is no answer at all. Let's hope the scan helps, but obviously my worry is that such a sudden deterioration is the prelude to even more difficult times.

Sorry to bring some gloom, although Chris is a little brighter this evening and the swelling in her left arm (the worst) does appear to have reduced today.

As you know, we are due our next holiday on 25th so we are hoping that she will improve over next two weeks in order that she can travel. The sun will do her good!

God bless,
Trevor & Chris xxx

6th November – Thoughts late at night

What is all this? Chris is really suffering with her swollen arms and legs. We talked about quality of life but what do I know? I'm not dying. She looks so very frail. So pale. Whiter shade of pale. She left looking just like a ghost. My love. She hurts and I can't fix it. Helpless. But I love her so I should be able to fix it. Control. Where is my fucking control now? Nowhere. She's strong but the pain is reducing her. Taking her away. Reducing her fight. Shall I just give in, go? We all scream, don't leave us. But it's up to Chris.

Tears pull at my eyelids as I think of the words to say. What about Ollie? Harriet? Will they remember? Or will Chris become a shapeless memory like my Gran? She's worth so much more.

This is the day that I really knew it was going to end. A coffin. A casket. Fine words. Emptiness. Loneliness. Nowhere Man. Self-pity. Weak. Tomorrow is a blank. No reason to carry on. So much for pleasing others ego.

Wish I could cry more. With Rob. Not Chris. Easy with Chris, we laugh and cry together.

Daft. Can't go on.

Drinking. To sleep. Crap excuse. Start smoking. Thinking about it. Why not? Who cares?

Will redouble healing efforts. Best wishes to you both.

Hx (Helen Leathers)

God bless you, Trev ... try to keep your spirits up and I hope the sun works its wonders. Love. (John Caruth)

God Bless you both.Keep strong.

Netty and Julian xxx (Turner)

Oh Trevor

I am so sorry – keep your spirits up and everyone informed – you are both in my prayers

Love Shirl (Hunter)

Dear Trevor,

Joyce and I send our best wishes and love to` you both. we do hope that Chris feels well enough to enjoy a forthcoming holiday. Her fortitude is wonderful,

Jim & Joyce (Williams)

Dear Trevor,

Thanks for your regular updates on Chris. I am so sorry to hear of this instability and the pain, stress and worry that goes with it, and I hope that the slight improvement you both noticed keeps on going.

Denise and I send you both our love and we just pray that Chris's CT scan will be positive and enable your trip to go ahead as you plan.

God bless you two too.

Tony (Wightman)

Thank you for keeping us informed about Christine. I often think of her and you and I am amazed how well you both have coped. I will say a few extra prayers for you both and pray she isn't in too much pain. Life is a bitch and plays some bad things to you.

Keep us informed, God bless you both.

Chrissy and Dickie (Probert)

Dearest Trevor and Chris,

So sorry to hear that Chris is having a tough moment, but glad to hear that perhaps the pain is easing now.

My thoughts are with you both as ever. That holiday will be just the best!

Lots of love,
Sue (Cameron)

Dear Friends,
You are having a rotten time and we can only think of you from afar. Just be sure the positive thoughts are pouring forth and if spirit is medicine then you two have buckets of it.

God be with you,
John and Florence (Oliver)

Hi Trevor,
I am thinking of you both and pray that she will be well enough to travel.

Take care,
Janet Peacock

Hi Trevor,
You are both in our thoughts right now, please give Chris all our love.
Jeff & Tina (Hull) xx

Dear Trevor,
You and Chris are in our prayers and thoughts...

Lots of love,
Carol & Gary (Milner)

Trevor,
Thanks for this, and I will continue to pray for you both.

Regards,
Dave (Tubby)

Hi Trev,
So sorry to hear that Chris is not doing so well, but hope that it is a temporary blip in her otherwise remarkable progress to-date.

We just got off the cruise ship in Athens so will send out a news letter later.

Love to you both,
Rowl and Hazel x (Charge)

Dear Trevor and Chris,

Thank you for the update. Chris, we certainly hope and pray that you will soon improve from your most recent treatment. We're sorry you feel so ill.

Albie has had a pretty rough few months. He had a stent implanted in the largest artery leading from the heart.He still has some angina chest pain, but the stent is working well. Then this week, he was diagnosed with a melanoma on his forehead. They removed a big piece of skin, but we don't have the pathology yet from the surrounding tissue. We pray for the best possible result.. Other than that, we are doing well and are now in Florida for the rest of the winter.

Now for the bright side. Albie's eldest grandaughter got married a few weeks ago in California. It was a little uncertain if he could travel, but we made it. My daughter came with us, and carried all the hand luggage, did the driving etc, so it was as easy as possible for us.

Trevor and Chris, we think of you often and about what a wonderful cruise we took with you. Keep in touch.

Love,
Miriam and Albie

Thinking of you both and continue to pray. Love and hugs to Chris.

With much love,
Janet x (Price)

Hi Trev,

So sorry to hear that Chris is going through a not so good patch at the moment, unfortunately, this is the nature of this terrible unforgiving beast of a disease. It is quite possible that she will pick up a little, Trev, well enough to enable you to enjoy your holiday. The time you two have away seems to work wonders for both of you, so I am sure you will be able to make the very best of it.

Keep strong Trevor it is a very rocky road and I know that at some point you will be managing the most challenging stage in this journey. Once you hit this point you will need even more support and help from those around you, and I hope that I will be strong enough to give you that support if and when you need it.

For me, I cannot begin to describe how I feel or how hard the past 4 weeks have been. I am a long way off from being 'back to normal' despite the fact life goes on and that I need to be focused both at work and at home. I have not called you as it would not be fair to share my feelings at this stage, I do not want to upset or distress you right now, and I know and appreciate that you need to stay focused and hopeful that Chris's final battle is still a long way off.

I send you all my love and prayers to both of you and hope that I will see you both after your holidays and before Christmas.

All my love and hope for you both,
Sian x x x x (Ayckbourn)

Hi Trev,
Thanks for keeping me updated. I'm a bit of a bloke when it comes to writing, but I always read your news and Chris and you are in my thoughts and prayers. I might even manoeuvre my calendar in the not too distant to call in and say hello. Promise to give you some decent notice first!

With best wishes,
Andrew (Hartley)

Dear Chris and Trevor,
Chris, we were so sorry to hear about the bad reaction you are having with your treatments. We are ever hopeful that this is just a temporary side-effect and will correct itself in time for your holiday in late November. We will look forward, as we have, to hearing about your trip.

We cannot express the admiration that we have for you both as you carry on through these most difficult times.

Your strength and courage is such that we feel small next to you.

As always, our thoughts and prayers are with you as you navigate through this latest hardship.

Love to you both,
Gary and Debbie (Murrish)

How to Dance in the Rain

It was a busy morning, about 8:30, when an elderly gentleman in his 80's arrived to have stitches removed from his thumb. He said he was in a hurry as he had an appointment at 9:00 am.

I took his vital signs and had him take a seat, knowing it would be over an hour before someone would be able to see him. I saw him looking at his watch and decided, since I was not busy with another patient, I would evaluate his wound. On exam, it was well healed, so I talked to one of the doctors, got the needed supplies to remove his sutures and redress his wound.

While taking care of his wound, I asked him if he had another doctor's appointment this morning. He said no, he needed to go to the nursing home to eat breakfast with his wife. I inquired as to her health. He told me she had been there for a while and that she was a victim of Alzheimer's disease. As we talked, I asked if she would be upset if he was a bit late. He replied she no longer knew who he was, she had not recognized him in five years now .I was surprised, and asked him, 'And you still go every morning, even though she doesn't know who you are?'

He smiled as he patted my hand and said, 'She doesn't know me, but I still know who she is.'

I had to hold back tears as he left, I had goose bumps on my arm, and thought, 'That is the kind of love I want in my life.'

True love is neither physical, nor romantic. True love is an acceptance of all that is, has been, will be, and will not be.

With all the jokes and fun that are in e-mails, sometimes there is one that comes along that has an important message. This one I thought I could share with you.

The happiest people don't necessarily have the best of everything; they just make the best of everything they have. I hope you share this with someone you care about. I just did.

'Life isn't about how to survive the storm, but how to dance in the rain'.

Thank you Trev,
How is Chris doing? I worry about her so much.

Shirl (Hunter)

Hi Trevor,
Another beautiful story - just loved it. Thank you for sharing - these stories are always so nice to read.

Thank you.
Love, Debbie (Murrish)

13th November 2009

Hi Deb yes,some of these are rather good. Chris is slightly better today. Her scan and xray results are ok. Some fluid in right lung but no tumours. Pancreas tumour unchanged in size,liver clear. Consultant put her on steroids for 1 week to build her up prior to cruise and hopefully relieve swelling and pain in her arms.

Take care,
Trev

Hi Trev,
So happy to hear Chris is doing better today - that is really good news. It sounds as though you can prepare for your cruise, which sounds wonderful, by the way. Please give Chris our love and best wishes - to you too, Trev.

Take care,
Debbie (Murrish)

14th November 2009

Hi Shirley,
Chris has had a rocky 2 weeks with swelling and pain her arms. However, the medics have been excellent – her oncology consultant, her G.P, the local nurses and the MacMillan nurses. She had 'emergency' scan and xray on Thursday, and yesterday we had a 20 minute telephone consultation with her oncology consultant. The scans were basically good news – the pancreatic tumour remaining unchanged, not growing. She has some fluid in her right lung, but no tumours appearing, although if fluid increases they will drain it away. Her liver is clear. There were no blood clots found.

Pancreatic cancer is highly likely to spread to either liver or lungs, or both, and cause blood clots so there was cause for relief.

They have decided it is likely the swelling and pain is being caused by a reaction to her chemotherapy (the drug Gemcitabine). So, Chris has been put on a course of steroids (12 tablets a day – jeez!) which should both alleviate swelling (and thus pain) and also build her up in order for us to go on our cruise next week (25th). We just hope some of the possible steroid side-effects can be avoided. No more chemotherapy until we return from cruise in early December (8th).

Hope your recovery is going well, are you planning to visit George and the family over Christmas or are they escaping the wet UK to visit you in sunny Texas?

Take care,
Trevor

Hi Trev,
Well it is good news that the cancer is contained – that is the main thing and I just know Chris has such a positive attitude that helps tremendously.

I am recovering nicely thank you and yes I will be making the trip to see my babies – I love being a Grandma – I arrive on Saturday December 19th and I will be going with them to Orlando Jan 1st and then home to Houston on Jan 4th so a nice little trip.

Keep your chin up boss – you can get through this!
Shirl (Hunter)

Dear Trevor and Chris,
So sorry to hear that the last lot of chemo has affected you Chris so badly. I do hope that by now, another week on, you are feeling better and that the swelling has subsided. We are also praying that you will be well enough to go on your cruise and are all lined up ready to meet you off the boat at Santa Cruz for lunch!

Keep us posted on progress

Lots of love,
Sue and Jim x x x (Cameron)

Hi Trevor & Christine,
Have been thinking of you both and just thought I'd send a quick e mail just to know I have not forgotten you.

Saw pictures of Rowl and Hazel's wedding and Christine you looked so well but I know looks can deceive.

I realise you have been through a rough patch recently. I do hope the NHS are doing their stuff.

It's great that you have been able to pack so much into this last year and I do believe that out of a negative a positive comes- I may have said that before.

You will have met some wonderful, exciting and eccentric people on your travels, seen some fabulous places and that's what makes life so interesting.

I can be such a stick in the mud at travelling to different places. I get to know places well and just feel so at home there. Miss my father's home now though and all the apples we used to have.

I have now bought Steve out of the house in Cardiff and I am slowly doing it up. Slow being the word. I love DIY but love socialising even more.

Life for me is fine, few hiccups along the way but take it all as it comes.

Thinking and praying for you both.

Lots of love,
Jane xx (Grandison)

22nd November

Two weeks of misery, followed by a week of hope. Steroids working but at what cost? Chris seems a little mad, but not really. She came to the pub with me tonight, what a celebration from our friends. Chris of course has drunk too much but at least she'll sleep.

WHEN THE ROSES BLOOM AGAIN

~ Laura Cantrell ~

~ When The Roses Bloom Again ~

My email of 23rd November covered everything over these weeks. Chris literally was unable to cut food on her plate, barely able to raise a fork to her mouth such was the pain in her arms.

I felt helpless and useless, when alone very distressed and frequently tearful about her condition. It never entered my head we were entering the end game of her miracle though. I just wanted her arms solved so we could go on holiday once again.

When her oncologist decided to use steroids I should have heeded the words of Kim Sharman more. He had told me that steroids were used for 'the last hurrah' in the case of cancer patients. I never viewed them in that way, believing if they solved her arm problems then they would be worth the discomfort Chris suffered with them. We also both underestimated the negative importance of the arrival of fluid in her lung. Ultimately, this is what 'got' her but neither of us, at this early stage, viewed it as anything to be too worried about. How wrong we were!

By now winter had arrived, it was cold, damp and miserable. Chris needed blue skies, sunshine and warmth.

Chemotherapy	*None*
November 12th	*CT scan*
November 12th	*Consultant: Oncologist (tele-consultancy)*
November 20th	*GP House Visit:*

Update No 10 – 23rd November 2009

Greetings,

Well, after a few scares in the last two/three weeks we set off tomorrow down to Southampton to stay overnight before embarking Wednesday on our latest holiday jaunt, a P&O cruise around The Canaries & Madeira. There have been times in the last few weeks we didn't believe we would be making this holiday, and I still have some reservations about whether Chris really is well enough to take the trip. She is much better, but I can tell she has been weakened by the latest difficulties she has encountered. Naturally, Chris will have none of that talk and has declared herself fit and ready to travel whilst hoping we don't have any rough weather after we set sail.

As I wrote on the 6th, Chris had developed swollen arms over weekend 31st Oct/ 1st Nov, too tender to touch and giving her great pain. This continued throughout the first 2 weeks of November. We had several visits from the District Nurse, MacMillan nurse and GP as well as a meeting with oncologist registrar. Her arms were too swollen and painful to have her weekly blood tests so she has had no chemotherapy since 30th Oct.

She had more scans and x-rays, followed by a 25 minute telephone consultation with her oncologist. He decided, in conjunction with her GP, to put her on steroids to reduce the swelling, which hopefully would also reduce pain. His main driving force was to get Chris fit enough to take our holiday – he is a great believer in 'quality of life' for his terminally ill patients. Steroids are a nasty word for cancer patients as they are often the last drug used in an effort to make a patient's last days more bearable – so we weren't exactly jumping about with happiness.

However, I'm pleased to say that this plan seems to have worked. The swelling has gone and her pain has reduced marginally each day. To put that in context, for the two weeks she was suffering it was impossible for her to cut a piece of meat and it was only just possible for Chris to lift a forkful of food to her mouth. Increased pain-killers didn't do much to help.

She has been taking TWELVE 5mg steroid tablets a day last week, this week reduced to TEN per day and then reducing downwards each week over the next four to five weeks. There can be side-effects (isn't there always!) but overall the benefits outweigh the downsides.

The good news from the scans was that there has been no real further spread. Chris has some slight fluid in her right lung, but suffers no breathlessness or breathing problems, and the change in her lower vertebrae bone make-up is also stable. The pancreatic tumour has not grown, neither has it got into her liver again (or anywhere else) so we must be grateful for the miracle that has taken place to keep her with us for almost a year, many months more than forecast.

After the awful wet weather of recent weeks, we are looking forward to a two week break that should give Chris some warm sun on her face. We just hope the recent storms do not attack us around the Bay of Biscay! We are meeting my cousin Susan in Tenerife for lunch on Dec 2nd – an amazing coincidence to be there at the same time. We're looking forward to seeing Madeira for the first time and I've promised Chris I'll take to her to Reids Hotel for afternoon tea. Very English!

We'll report back on return. Thank you for the many emails and calls we have received in the last couple of weeks. As I hope you know, they are really important to us and help us continue to focus on maximizing the fight. Likewise, those of you who can visit – we love to see you, Chris particularly so, as she sometimes tires of me being Mother Hen! (We have had a smashing lunch with my old customers from B'ham, Brian and Pat Bourne, a wonderful day with Peter and Val Halman, who came up from Wargrave, Peter being one of our first bosses at Cadburys about 45 years ago! – followed later that week with lunch with Barry and Carol Lawton).

All our love and thanks for being with us on the journey,
Trevor & Chris – Global Travellers in extremis!
xxx

Hi you two,
Just got back from two weeks away ourselves, in Egypt. The warm weather has served us both very well and we know that you will both benefit getting away from this (let's be frank!) bloody shambolic British weather! Sue and I wish you both a lovely holiday and within a few days of being in the lovely warm sunshine you will both feel a lot more relaxed. Enjoy every minute of your holiday, we will both be thinking of you.

Sorry this is a brief communication, just got back from the office and need to turn a few things around before a ludicrously early start to be in Morrison's Head Office tomorrow morning! I changed job in the summer and between that and training incredibly hard for the Abingdon Marathon last month (finally breaking that elusive 3 hour barrier!) we have not managed to pop in and see you both. Apologies.

Let us know once you return to these windswept and rather damp shores and we will arrange to visit for a cup of tea or two!

Take care, God bless and enjoy.
Paul and Sue (Blake)

Hi Trev,
Thanks for the latest report. It's great to see that Chris is still fighting back. You two

be sure to have a great cruise.We've no doubt the sun will do you both a power of good.Look forward to seeing you at Ombersley on the 13th December.

Love,
Rob and Aud (Wilson)

Hello Trev,
Please give Chris our love and tell her that we are thinking of her and wish her a wonderful trip. We'll talk soon.

Geoff (Owens)

God bless both and pray you have the strength to enjoy your so deserved holiday.
Julian and Annette (Turner)
x x x x

Hi Trev,
Marvellous - have a great time.

All the best,
Ken (Lewis)

Hi Trev and Chris,
Just to say again, from us both, have a wonderful time in The Canaries and Madeira. We will be thinking of you both and hope all goes well. We look forward to our usual Christmas celebrations when you are back and to seeing some of your pictures of your holiday.

With much love from us both,
Rowl and Hazel xx (Charge)

Hi Chris & Trevor,
I'm glad you are feeling a bit better and the swelling has gone down. Have a fantastic holiday, I hope the sun shines for you. I will definitely catch up with you when you get back.

Thinking of you. Lots of love,
Andrea (Stephens) xxxxx

Trev,
Thanks for the updates. Hope you both have a great time on your cruise. Thinking of you.

Cheers,
Nick, Sarah, Harry and George (Brown)

Thank you for this update, Trevor, and I hope you are able to have a really special time away together.

God bless,
Dave (Tubby)

To Trevor and Christine,
So pleased to hear that you will be taking your holiday cruise as planned. I'll be over to see you when you get back, to hear all about it. May God watch over you and heal you.

Much love,
Janet xx

We are off to the States early Monday not back until 29th December. Do hope you made the best of your cruise and generally enjoyed it although not up to Victoria's standards! Do hope Chris is still better side out. Give her a big hug from both of us, and we wish you both a Happy and Peaceful Christmas and ditto for the New Year.

John & Betty (Edmundson)

I'm very biased, but I think Chris looks utterly serene and beautiful in this photo, taken on Arcadia just six or seven weeks before she passed away (November 2009)

I'll Come Running

~ James Taylor ~

Chris is still radiant, still smiling, even though this photo on Arcadia was taken just six weeks before she passed away.It is the last photo we ever had taken together - it means a lot that she was still doing pretty well. (December 2009)

~ I'll Come Running ~

Our cruise was enjoyable but Chris was not as well for this one as she was earlier in the year. We met several nice people - Mike and Pauline Gibbons in particular - but the weather wasn't as good as we had hoped.

Chris had been very very slowly deteriorating during the cruise, her chest marginally worsening throughout the two weeks. Not enough to cause serious worry but enough that I was aware of the changes. In her usual style Chris treated this slight worsening with contempt, enjoying the holiday. Our high spot was probably meeting cousin Susan in Tenerife for lunch. I wheeled Chris in her wheelchair off the ship and into Santa Cruz where a good time was had by all. It's nice that Sue and Jim's lasting memory is of the real Chris, sat in sunshine drinking beer and eating salad with a smile. That lunch became important in my memories as things transpired.

You will be staggered to learn that I spent 30 minutes in the gym every day, plus embarking on a detoxification programme! During that programme I met Brian Moore, an inspirational character who was also terminally ill. Brian died in March this year (2010), a lovely man of great faith. Why do the good die young?

Chris simply wasn't well enough to enjoy the cruise as much as before. We spent the days quietly together, enjoying each other's company and at ease with ourselves. Looking back now it was almost as though we knew instinctively we were coming to the end of our great adventure, although it never felt that way.

Our evenings were spent in the company of Mike and Pauline, new friends from Essex and Chris enjoyed a good few large Cointreaus in the two weeks. She never changed, love her!

When we returned home she began to worsen. One of our GPs visited on 15th December, and I wish I had made him admit her to hospital. Maybe her lung wouldn't have collapsed. We waited to see the oncologist on the 18th, but saw one of his registrars who couldn't get her admitted that day. She told us to go to New Cross, Wolverhampton on Monday 21st. Chris was very poorly indeed, and my concerns are reflected in my 18th December email.

The weekend of 19th/20th was our worst. Chris was desperately poorly, so weak from the effort of breathing that we had to use the wheelchair to move her around the house. She wasn't interested in food. I had her brother Robert – our strongest support – come to stay with her Sunday whilst I scouted out New Cross Hospital. The weather was terrible, snow and ice, and I didn't want us to be in the wrong place when we arrived on the Monday morning.

| December 18th | Consultant: Oncologist Registrar |
| December 15th | GP House Visit: |

Christmas Report on Chris – Update No 11 – 18th December 2009

I am afraid this is not a 'good news' update. Chris really is very poorly. We are at our lowest ebb for some time. I pray that the hospital on Monday – see lower part of email – is able to be more positive. Chris is struggling for the first time but maybe the emotional pressures of Christmas are not helping.

Hi,

When I began sending out update reports on Chris, I thought that there would only be four or five to send, so bad was her initial diagnosis. It was only in my dreams that I thought I would be sat here in December writing yet another one. To be writing this, No 11, is a miracle. All the love, all the prayers, all the positive thoughts, the distance healing, all the belief we have received from our friends and families combined with Chris's inner strength mean that despite Chris's condition, 2009 has, in many ways, been not a sad year but a very happy year! A very humble 'thank you' to everyone.

It is impossible to put into words how positive the effect has been to receive so many phone calls, emails, visits, letters and cards telling us we are in your thoughts and prayers. We are truly 'living a miracle' as neither of us thought she would be here for this Christmas. Well, I say that, but Chris has always set herself the target of making her 60th birthday on December 27th. She is amazing, simply refusing to accept her condition as diagnosed by the medical fraternity, telling everyone who asks how she is that 'I'll be alright'!

A great example of her strength was a comment she made on our recent Canaries cruise. We reckon 90% of the passengers were older than us and there were many in wheelchairs, disabled etc. As I ruminated laying by the swimming pool, looking around one day, that there was little to look forward to in old age when I saw these old buggers Chris, studying a couple of severely disabled individuals, said – quite casually – that really there were plenty of people worse off than her! It is a wonderful example of her positive outlook. She does have her bad days, which upset me because they are so out of character for her that I worry twice as much, but she is dealing with everything so well I cannot tell you how proud she makes me and how privileged I am to love her.

Our cruise around The Canaries was a nice break, probably better for me than Chris. The weather was disappointing – only two really hot days - but we met my cousin for a terrific lunch together in Santa Cruz on Tenerife. The ship – P&O Arcadia – was not in the same class as Queen Victoria but we met some lovely people, and made new friends in Mike and Pauline from Essex, with whom we put the world to rights every evening. We've made some of our best friends on holiday, and so it was lovely to continue that tradition with them. You will be stunned to learn that I spent 30 mins every day in the gym on the fitness bike as I began another futile attempt to do regular exercise for the first time in 40 years!

We went out to dinner with friends last Friday, but I had to bring Chris home after a couple of hours as she simply couldn't cope any longer. Since then, I am keeping her indoors (sounds a bit like prison, doesn't it?). The weather has worsened and I am very worried about infection, with the ever-present danger of pneumonia. I'm probably being completely paranoid – I've just suffered a heavy cough and cold and it's a surprise I haven't emigrated, I've been so scared about passing it to her – but better safe than sorry. Aside from chest pain, she continues to be weak but worst of all, we are having to increase her morphine to keep the pain to some sort of bearable level. The side effects of morphine can be both amusing and frightening, as it changes her character. It makes her a little confused and edgy, and less able to cope with anything out of the ordinary. She is fine when we have visitors, less able to cope when away from home (as per last Friday). Morphine also adversely affects her memory, so we often have the same conversation repeated.

However, the point of this update is sadly to let you know that since Update 10 (and last week), unfortunately, Chris has taken a turn for the worse. She was not particularly well on holiday but she is now suffering very severe chest pain due to having approx 4 litres of fluid in her right lung/chest area. I am taking her to New Cross Hospital, Wolverhampton on Monday where we expect them to admit her in order to drain her lungs/chest of that fluid. Fortunately her breathing is 99% ok, so she isn't classified as an emergency (although it seems an emergency to me!). Sadly, this development has been caused as a direct result of the cancer breaking down her defences – effectively a spread of the cancer – and so this build-up of fluid is likely to keep repeating. Obviously we won't know the full prognosis until next week but we ask for even more of your prayers, healing and positive thinking over the next few days.

We continue our plans for Christmas when we are having Chris's Mum over, and Robert, Pippa and the children are arriving Christmas afternoon to stay for a few days. Unbelievably, I am in charge of Christmas Lunch and I will furnish you with my menu in the next few days! Pretentious or what! Christmas is likely to be an emotional time for the family and I am just a bit twitchy because I have always felt bad vibrations about this Christmas ever since Chris was diagnosed. I just hope I'm wrong and will be proved to be a negative so and so..

All that remains is to wish you and your family a Happy Christmas and a healthy and successful 2010. Thanks once again for your support throughout this difficult year, please make some special prayers for Chris over this weekend as I am very worried for her.

God bless.
Trevor & Chris
xxx

Hi chum,
Thanks for the update. Glad the holiday went ok despite the weather but clearly in no small way to the new friends you've both made.

Totally understand how you must feel as Chris is now having to deal with pain caused by fluid on the lungs, and so yes we will be putting in the extra positive thoughts and prayers over this weekend. May her guardian angel work her magic again!

Our love and support to you both and our very best wishes for your joint well being this Christmas.

Yours aye,
Tony (Wightman)

Hi Trev,
This is not such great news although I'm glad that the cruise was a success. Keep me posted next week Trev because Ali and I would very much like to visit over Christmas and for the 1st year in 25 I have a whole week off so we were going to try and come up, but that's only if Chris is up to it.

Love to you both and hopefully the news isn't too negative on Monday.
David & Ali (Stephens)

Dear Trev & Chris,
We are so sorry to hear that things are not so good and we are thinking of you a lot.
We will look forward to seeing you both on the 27th as planned.

Love
Rowl & Hazel x (Charge)

Oh Trev all I can say is stay strong.
Love Shirl (Hunter)

Hi again Trev,
I am in Washington airport trying to beat a snow storm heading for Manchester and
my grandbabies - if you need help with anything I will be at Georgina's - her mobile
number is xxx and my Blackberry is xxx just call me and I will help. I will be home until
Jan 1st.

Please give my love to Chris.
Shirl (Hunter) xx

Hi Trevor
Thanks for the update on Chris. You are in our thoughts mate.

Kind regards,
Roy (James)

Thanks Trevor, for the update.
You remain in our prayers at this time, in particular on Monday as you go to New
Cross.

I hope you are able to both have a fantastic Christmas together, and enjoy every
moment as you have been the last 11 months.

God bless,
Dave (Tubby)

I am sure you will gets loads of responses but here is another one!

Christmas is that time for families and we both pray that you will enjoy yours together.
Forget the chef bit and have a Chinese carry out!

Chris is astonishing but we won't forget the old man in this. You have kept us all in touch and have given her the most amazing year. Life is for living and you have both done that to the full in 2009.

We wish you and your family the closest and best Christmas ever and we will just take it a day at a time.

John and Florence (Oliver)

Hi to you both,
It's always helpful to hear your news.

As you say it's wonderful that you were both able to have such an enjoyable time on the cruise.

Marilyn and I have just returned from shopping at Tesco in Handforth, so I thought I'd have a cup of tea and do e-mails before hitting the sack.

I'm in Manchester tomorrow with a friend of mine watching Sunderland beat City!!!

We both send you all our love and best wishes for Christmas, and be assured that you are in our prayers every night.

God bless,
Dave & Marilyn (Dippie)

Thinking of you and praying (along with my church in Worcester) for healing.

Love Janet

Hope to pop in to see you on 27th.

As usual, thank you for sending the update report on Chris. Both Carol and I think and talk about you two very often and I just want to say what I always say, which is that you are both very much in our thoughts and prayers.

I have been thinking quite a lot about the meaning of life and what's it all about, etc etc... Normally, when you're in the sphere of full-time working, you of course have very little time to think about anything other than just getting through with the working role etc, but a number of people who are close to me have been suffering ill health - and this just gets you thinking. Also, when I'm on one of my week-long business trips (as I am at the moment) I get thinking about such things as:

– What's the point of it all (working I mean)?

– Where am I going (spiritually)?

– What will I do when my working life comes to an end?

All very deep I hear you asking yourself. Well you would also be a little crazy if you had spent (as I have), 1 week in Tokyo. We had our year end/ budgetary meeting here in Japan – with all of the usual quirky ways our Japanese colleagues have of doing things. I now know that I have become a little Japanese myself – because I heard some new colleagues from a company that we have acquired saying how odd this and that was, when I was thinking to myself 'it's perfectly normal'??

Anyway, 1 week in Tokyo is more than enough. This will make you laugh – by the time you wake up (and assuming that you read this on Saturday AM), I'll be with my previous boss making a presentation to 40+ top business managers from Mitsubishi Chemical Corporation. The elite of Mitsubishi are on a week-long training course, and the high-light of their week will be yours truly making a presentation. The part about failing my 12+ exams doesn't really get a mention!!!

Wish me luck? I'll call you when (if) I ever get back.

Regards,
Gary (Milner)

PS: It was beautiful this morning – I can just see Mount Fuji in the distance from my hotel room. We had a look around the Royal Palace – have a look at the attached.

Dear Chris and Trevor,
So sorry to receive today's e-mail and hear that you are feeling so unwell Chris. We can only pray that the hospital on Monday can do something to alleviate the pain.

We think about you all the time and send you our love and prayers and hope you will be well enough to enjoy Christmas and your 60th.

It has finally stopped raining up here. It is very cold and frosty but at last there is some sunshine too. We are in Scotland for Christmas but hoping to go to Wales for New Year. So we will keep in touch as to whether there is any possibility of a flying visit.

Lots and lots of love,
Sue and Jim x x x (Cameron)

Give Chris a big hug from Betty and John currently in South Carolina. Wish her a happy birthday next week!

John (Edmundson)

Hi Trev and Chris,
Greetings from Australia!

Thanks again for your regular updates - we really appreciate being kept up-to-date, and we have a sense of shared victory with every update. I know it's been a tough year for you guys and our thoughts have never been far from your battle. In fact, it's not overstating the case to say that you've both provided inspiration to us, for our relatively minor dips and bumps.

It amazes us that you guys have fitted so much into 2009! After all your travels, it sounds like a quiet Christmas with family will be a holiday in itself!

We loved hearing about your luxury cruises and exotic holiday locations (no we didn't really – we were bloody jealous!). The closest we got to a luxury cruise was we hired a houseboat on the Murray River for a week (see photos). No it wasn't the Mediterranean, and it was hardly the Queen Vic, but good fun nevertheless. Until I ran it aground, that is! I steadfastly maintain it was not my fault that the river level changed overnight, leaving us stranded on the bank, then waiting hours for a much larger vessel to come along and haul us off in a stunning naval manoeuvre (imagine two elephants copulating on ice-skates). I had no idea what I was doing and was lucky not to seriously damage the boat, but now of course, I see it as the biggest laugh of the year.

But we've had a strong sense this year that these are just minor dips and bumps. And it's your updates that have provided the perspective. We were tremendously impressed with your reflection that this has been a good year - there's a lot of learning in that comment for us. And we've shared that with the boys.

We are still sending our most positive thoughts and hopes for you both. We are very keen to hear you've had a wonderful family Christmas, celebrated Chris's birthday in style, and overcome this latest hurdle. In fact, we're getting used to hearing about you overcoming setbacks and expect to hear more!

So we wish you an especially memorable and meaningful Christmas, and more importantly, that you tackle 2010 with the same strength and determination.

Our very best wishes to you both.

Cheers,
Tim (MacLachlan

Hi Trev,
Hope that you are ok and Chris is battling on in true trooper style!

Bec forwarded me your update and I just thought I'd drop you a quick email with a possible suggestion to help Chris build up her immunities over the winter period. Coconut oil. It is an absolutely unbelievable product and I have been working with this genius nutritionalist over the past few years who has done a lot of research into many, many products and totally swears by it for the building up of immunity. It's antiviral and antibacterial and is one of the only other sources of the same nutrients that breast milk (which obviously is used to build up babies!) and is high in levels of good saturated fats which makes up the majority of every cell wall in our bodies. It is completely natural and if you buy organic and fair trade then you are on to a winner! I mix it with butter or use it instead of oil when I cook or mix it into porridge, etc.

Anyway, it was just something I thought you might want to look in to and see if it might be of use in Chris's diet to help her a little - no worries if not but I thought I'd email you none the less !

See you soon,
Lucy (Jackson)

PS If you want anymore info on any other products I will gladly ask my colleague. He is extremely forward thinking and very knowledgeable and you never know eh !

PPS I hope you don't think I'm interfering, just wanted to pass the info on if it helps

Hi Trevor,
Thanks for the update. Thinking of you both - I hope you can enjoy Christmas together.

Best wishes,
Bob (Sprot)

Hello to you both,
Sorry to hear Chris not too good, we will have to meet up for a drink. We keep saying it but never do it. Celia says to say hello. I hope you both have a good Xmas

Love from Reg and Helen (Wheeler)

We were pleased but apprehensive when we received your email and then sorry to hear Chris has been in such great pain. You are both so brave, Chris for her suffering and you Trevor for watching someone you love going through so much.

We sincerely hope your Christmas will be spent in happiness with all your family and Chris will spend it as free of pain as possible.

We will be thinking of, and praying for, you both.

Our love and best wishes.
Pat and Brian (Bourne)

Trevor & Chris,
Thanks for the update, we will be thinking of you both and especially you cooking lunch Trevor.

Both take care,
Janet & Richard (Peacock)

Dear Trevor,
Thank you for your newsy email.

I am so pleased Chris has had these extra months with you, what a blessing. She is a very brave lady and your email made me cry. We do hope you manage to enjoy your family Christmas. We have had a sad year with the loss of Paul's mum and my daughter in law's father so we know the importance of family. My prayers are as ever with you.

Fondest regards
Clare (Farrands).

Dear Trevor,
Thank you for including me in the list of people you send these updates to. When I received the first one I was a little surprised as I had not met Chris (the day I visited your house she was sleeping), and it seemed a very personal account to be sharing with someone you had met in business.

However reading each update has been incredibly inspiring, not only through learning the strength of Chris's character and the positive determination not to be beaten by her illness, but also to understand the very special relationship the two of you share and the strength of your character through this difficult time. It is apparent that you have played a significant part in Chris continuing way beyond the original prognosis, you are a good man who deserves a very big pat on the back. (I hope that doesn't sound patronising.)

I truly hope and pray that you both have a great Christmas.

Best regards,
Stephen (Barclay)

Hi Trevor & Chris,
Thank you for the latest e-mail and your best wishes for Christmas and 2010.

We are so sorry to receive one that is not so upbeat as usual about how Chris is progressing. We wish her all the very best for this week's hospital visit and hope that she will be back well enough to enjoy Christmas and her birthday.

It has been quite inspirational to receive the regular reports and to see how positive and strong Chris is and how you are both living each moment so positively.

I have spoken to Sue since you met her and Jim in Tenerife and she has said how wonderful it was to see you both for the lunch and how well she thought Chris was doing.

Good luck with the gym regime, hope you can continue with it! I can appreciate the effort you made as I have probably not been near one for 40 years as well (and should). Hope you are over your cold now and improving.

Judy and I will be having her parents down for Christmas as usual and although the two girls have left home and are establishing their own they should have both back here for Christmas day at least. Unfortunately Jo has to work the following day and her boyfriend is on the 12-hour night shifts right across the Christmas period (he is an ambulance technician, training to be a paramedic) so we will see some of him when he is not asleep. Helen will be home for the day and then she will be joining her boyfriend at his relatives in Bristol.

Anyway, Chris will be in our thoughts and prayers this week. Have a wonderful Christmas and 60th birthday and looking forward to positive reports in 2010.

Lots of love,
Rob and Judy (Price)

Hi Trevor,

I read your emails with both interest and concern for Chris and I print them off for Dad! You are very good about it all and I wish you both as good a Christmas as you can manage and my thoughts are always with you.

Cheers,
Ian (Fletcher-Price)

Dear Trevor and Chris,
So happy to hear from you, and thank you so much for your warm good wishes for the holiday season.

Chris, thank you for the update about your health. We wish you the longest and happiest life that is possible for you. Enjoy your family for the holidays. That is exactly what we intend to do in Florida. Our gang starts to arrive tomorrow, and they'll all be here by Thursday. We hope that the weather lives up to their expectations, as they love to be outdoors after traveling from the cold and snow.

Keep on writing,
Love Miriam and Albie

Hi to you both,
Well only 2 days to go and Christmas will be upon us all. It makes me smile every time I think of you all being together on Christmas Day after being told it most probably wouldn't happen. Your strength as a couple to cope with the past year as you have makes me so proud, I'm pretty sure I wouldn't have coped half as well.

Mum has mentioned they are travelling to you for Christine's 60th, weather permitting. We are so sorry we can't join them, it would have been lovely to see you all again. unfortunately we have no-one to leave the kids with and due to Dean's leg still not being sorted out he is unable to sit in a car for more than an hour. He is due to get his steroid injection on 27th Jan and we are hoping that will be an end to his problem. If not an operation is the next option.

All that remains to say is that we wish you both a wonderful and peaceful Christmas, and we hope you have a lovely 60th birthday Aunty Christine. Our thoughts and prayers are with you both and we will be raising a glass to you on Christmas Day.

With all our love as always,
Lesley, Dean, James and Lewis xxxx (Carpenter)

Waiting On A Friend

~ The Rolling Stones ~

The family - Pippa, Robert, Hattie, Granny, Grandad and Ollie - in Church Lane, Bewdley (February 2009)

~ Waiting On A Friend ~

On the morning of the 21st December, Chris was really poorly. She was disorientated and for the first time I was unable to cope. In tears, I phoned MacMillan (Nursing)who arranged for the district nurses to come up to wash and dress her. It was the first time that I ever felt that we were not in control of our own destiny. The journey to the hospital was quiet, Chris really not 'with it' and in obvious pain. I was in a minor panic, disturbed and uncertain where we were heading.

Wrong entrance at hospital, I had to wheel Chris in her wheelchair, in sub-zero temperatures, around the outside of the hospital to the correct location. As usual, no complaints from her about my incompetence. We were told to wait in the waiting room, but after 20 minutes I was back at reception. 'I think you need to get my wife seen to', I said, 'Otherwise she is going to die in your waiting room.' 2 minutes later the sister is there, we are into a sideward and Chris is hooked up to oxygen. She was to be on oxygen for most of the remaining days of her life.

We were there five hours while they conducted tests as part of admittance assessment. The ward sister took twenty minutes to complete her paperwork, then we were finally waiting for the porters to take Chris to the cancer ward. Chris had been so brave all day, calm and accepting, but she remained very disorientated and anxious. We put this down to the increased morphine and the natural worry of entering hospital. Little did we realise.

Once in the cancer ward we were assured that when her chest drain was set up we would see an immediate improvement. Finally, eight hours after we arrived at the hospital the chest consultant arrived to fit her drain. For the first time that day I relaxed a little. It is impossible to overstate the feeling of helplessness I felt all day. Chris had been in pain and distressed, and it was the first time we had really encountered the cancer as an evil disease that could kill her.

We knew it could (and probably would) but it always felt a remote probability because Chris had dealt with everything so well. This was different. She was really ill. Once she was set up with the drain I went home. Through the snow and ice. I felt utterly alone and cried throughout that night.

22nd December

When I returned the next afternoon it was to a problem. Despite a lot of fluid being drained there was no improvement in Chris. She was still in pain, still on oxygen and still disorientated. The cancer ward doctor was concerned and a little confused. They thought air was trapped between her fluid filled lung and her chest cavity. She needed suction to help relieve it and they were going to move her to the respiratory ward that evening. This was also disappointing because we had been told to expect an immediate improvement when the fluid was drained.

I followed her transfer to the new ward. Chris was suffering but not apparently in any great pain. Just discomfort. She ate little tea (I was thrown out at meal times) and I left that evening unhappy but comforted by the fact she was being well cared for in the correct ward.

23rd December

It doesn't feel like Christmas at all. The weather is lousy, snow and ice with sub-zero temperatures. We are told that there is no way Chris can be home for Christmas. The drain isn't working and the suction doesn't seem to be helping either. We are both upset but not surprised. Chris remains disorientated, slightly out of it and I am as concerned about this as I am about the lack of success with the drain. Chris herself has moments of great clarity and is able to communicate, not always making sense but always with humour. God, I love her.

Update 12 – 23rd December 2009

Hi,

Happy Christmas!

A brief update on Chris and sadly not a good one.

She is in Ward D20 of New Cross Hospital, Wolverhampton, which is a respiratory ward. She has been in the cancer ward previously for three days. I took her in on Monday, where they admitted her to have fluid drained from her right lung. This has been taking place over the last 48 hours but no improvement in her condition has been forthcoming. The doctors believe she may have air trapped between her lungs and chest, and this could be the reason she is unable to breathe without oxygen. She has been moved to a respiratory ward in order to be placed on suction, which is designed to gently remove the trapped air.

We have been told that whilst her cancer caused the build-up of fluid (and there may be still more bad news with this), this current problem is a respiratory issue and not a cancer issue. This at least gives us short-term hope.

It all means that Chris will remain in hospital for the immediate future. Our plans for Christmas and her 60th birthday have been broken and we are now just taking it day by day. She is in the best place, the doctors know what they are doing and she is receiving kind treatment. I visit every day from 2.30 and stay for as long as I am allowed. Chris has her eyes closed most of the time (probably out of boredom with me), but she is terribly tired (exhausted, really) by the effort of breathing.

These are dark and difficult days after our exciting year, but we remain hopeful that Chris will be home before long.

Enjoy Christmas and the festive season with your loved ones. Enjoy every moment because, as we well know, it can be snatched from us in a moment.

God bless,
Trevor & Chris
xxx

Trevor,
Thank you for the update. We are praying for Chris and for you. Faith says this is not the end, it is the beginning of something much better.

'For I am convinced that neither death nor life, neither angels nor demons, neither the present nor the future, nor any powers, neither height nor depth, nor anything else in all creation, will be able to separate us from the love of God that is in Christ Jesus our Lord' – *Romans* 8:38

Whatever happens, Trevor, God is for you and Chris and loves you both. In his big plan, there is a reason for all this, but it may not be obvious now.

Love and prayers,
Julian (Owens)

Hi Trevor,

Thanks for the update and sorry to hear that Christmas won't have the same feel about it this year. I've been doing my fair bit of hospital visits these last few months with my Mum with Alzheimers and my Dad recently diagnosed with colon cancer so I can empathise at least in a small way. I was hoping to try to call in today on my way down to Bristol to collect my mother-in-law, but weather, re-arranged timings and general weight of traffic meant it was impossible. I will be doing the return trip either on Tuesday or Thursday next week and will give you a call to see if you are able to share a coffee.

In the meantime, best wishes to you and Chris. My prayers are with you.
Andrew (Hartley)

Trevor,

Could you please send my love to Chris and give her a big Christmas kiss and cuddle from us all. It sounds like you are doing a fantastic job, thanks for the e-mails you have been sending as my thoughts are always with you all.

Love
Simon Lauren Alex Oliver and Lucas (Brown)

Hi Chris & Trev,

Really sorry to hear things have got worse, Leigh's dad has cancer and he had what sounds like a similar build up of fluid on his lungs. They drained it down and pumped him full of steroids and his condition did improve, so hope fully your Christmas plans will only be postponed not cancelled!!!

I have spent my fair share of time in hospital with Charlotte feeling helpless and sometimes hopeless, so if you ever passing and want a cup of tea and a chat please do.

All our thoughts are with you both at this Christmas time, hope to see you both soon!!

Love
Martin & Leigh (Loynes)

Hi Trev,

I opened this one with trepidation but you are both unbelievable with your positive attitude. I spent Xmas in hospital once and certainly the staff and visitors will make it as special as they can for both you and Chris - and you will probably get a personal visit from Santa and carol singers - something you wouldn't get at home!

Well sweetheart I know there will be a huge number of prayers and thoughts for both of you over the next few days and I will say a special one for you when I go to the midnight service tonight and I will light my candle as a sign of light and hope for you.

Sending you big hugs and kisses

God bless
Chrisy xxxxx (Cross)

Trev you are a good soul and Chris will know that in her heart ... you are in my prayers (I do still say my prayers!) and keep your strength up.

Love to you both.
John (Caruth)

Hi Trevor,
Sorry to hear the further news of Chris, please give her our love.

Hope the weather is not making your journeys to Wolverhampton too difficult, I'm sure that she appreciates your visits really!

Thank you for your best wishes for Christmas and the New Year, I hope that yours will just be delayed slightly and that Chris will be home again soon.

Wishing you and your loved ones all the very best

Love
Rob & Judy (Price)

Hi Trev,
Thanks for the latest update. I can't begin to imagine how difficult these times must be for you. Whatever happens you have both done tremendously well.

Our thoughts are with you

Love,
Rob and Aud (Wilson)

Trevor please convey our love; we are all saying a prayer.

Love
Julian and Netty x x x x (Turner)

Hi Trevor,
We will be thinking of you both over Christmas.

I hope you get the best time you can.

Catch up with you soon.
Paul & Fiona (Bradford)

Trevor,
I am sorry to hear Chris is struggling with the breathing, and I send my best wishes to you all at a very worrying time.

I know about draining the lungs, which normally does alleviate the breathing once the fluid is taken off, and you do get very tired trying to breath, so hopefully the rest and oxygen allows Chris to gain some strength and you can have some quality time together at Christmas.

My best wishes to you all.
Kevin (Fay)

Trevor,
You are a remarkable man; I have so much admiration for you!

My thoughts are with both of you and I wish you a Happy Christmas.

Love to the rest of the family.

Regards,
Lindsay (Townend)

Thinking of you and Chris.
Martin (Davies)

Hi Trevor,
We have been following the reports on Chris which have shown us how much you have tried to keep active and positive during these very difficult times and how much enjoyment and pleasure you have shared. Please pass on our best wishes to Chris

when you next see her and tell her we are thinking of her. We hope she will be home for Xmas as we know how much it will mean to both of you and the family.

Our prayers and thoughts are with you both.
Steve & Chris (Russell)

Hi Trevor,
Our thoughts and prayers will be with Chris, you and your family over the festive period.

Merry Christmas. All our best wishes,
Jeff & Tina xx (Hull)

I am so sorry Trev –stay strong
Shirl (Hunter)

Hi Trevor, thanks for the latest update, we are thinking of you and Chris all the time. We'll pray twice tonight. All our love, Have as happy a Christmas as circumstances will allow.

John & Betty (Edmundson)

Hi Uncle Trevor, we are so sorry to hear such worrying news, we think of you every day and pray that Aunty Christine will be able to come home soon. Please know that our thoughts and love are with you both. Please give Aunty Christine our love when you see her tomorrow. Our wish for you both is the best Christmas you can have under the circumstances, I'm sure the hospital staff will pull out all the stops.

With much love from
Lesley, Dean, James and Lewis xx (Carpenter)

Hello Trevor,
Sean and I will remember you and Chris in our prayers at mass on Christmas Day.

Love,
Liz and Sean (Forde) xx

Dear Trevor,
I am so sorry to hear the news that you and Chris will not be at home for Christmas. I am sure all of your friends are praying and thinking of you and if we all had a Christmas wish it would be for you and Chris to be at home celebrating Christmas and Chris's birthday.

It is little consolation for both of you but I have to tell you that in the past year you have through your own bravery and love been an inspiration and a constant reminder of living life to the full and what is truly important in life.

All our prayers and thoughts are with you both.

Best regards
Keith (Fleming)

God bless you both, be strong. Our thoughts are with you.

All our love,
Paul & Sue x (Blake)

Hi Trevor,
I'm sorry that you're going through a similar process with Chris to that I went through with Stef although inevitably with differences. At least you've been able to do things that you may not have done without this last year together. Certainly, Stef took the opportunity to explore the world- 2 trips to Israel on his own, Australia with me 3 years ago for 2 Ashes Test Matches (we lost all 5 matches if you remember) and Poland with a friend.

Chris and Stef are evidently both fighters. At the start of his treatment, Stef was told that only about 50% of patients survive the 3 months of chemo. He sailed through it with no side effects. So much so that he demanded a refund from his consultant of the £1.98 he spent on 2 buckets which he bought from B & Q because he was told that the chemo would make him be sick! Even in adversity, he was able to make a joke of it.

I only seem to remember Stef having his chest drained once but the improvement was dramatic; not surprising really when they removed something like 8 litres of fluid!

After the various procedures, he was always interested in what they did to him, whether it was the chest drain (he wanted to know what colour the fluid was!) or the stents inserted in his oesophagus. It was ever thus, from the 2 previous times he had contracted and survived cancers, a knee joint replacement in 2003, treatment for Carpel Tunnel syndrome in both wrists, knee ligament operations and broken legs. He really went through the mill. I, on the other hand (as my late GP and Godfather once said) am 'disgustingly healthy'. Stef never complained about his lot; never asked 'why me?'. I don't think I could be as stoical as he was.

A few days ago, I came across your text to me after Stef's funeral. I'd had no idea that Chris was as ill as she was. As you say I miss him a lot, not being able to talk football or cricket (or sport generally).

I got my dates wrong; we are at home on the 6th of January and then at Old Trafford for the return. Stef WILL always be there because I scattered some of his ashes under his seat at the Derby Match last season (as I did at the original Old Trafford during the cricket season).

I hope you both have a Merry Christmas (but not in the alcoholic sense).

Keep in touch (as Stef ALWAYS said to me).
Dan (Usansky)

Best wishes to both of you. Our thoughts are with you and we wish you strength and endurance.

Speak soon,
Love from Ewout, Hayley, Willem, and Anjes (van der Kleijn)

Love to both of you on Christmas Day, thinking of you always, hope Chris is feeling comfortable XXX
Steve & Jackie (Hickman)

Hi Trevor,
I'm so sorry to hear Chris won't be home for Christmas and probably her birthday, but yes, as you said she is in the best place. Please send her my love and tell her she is constantly in my thoughts.

Wish Robert, Pippa, Oliver and Hattie a 'Merry Christmas' from us.

See you soon

Lots of love,
Andrea (Stephens) xxxx

Love to you both thinking of you and praying for you both.
Love Janet

Hello Trev,
So sorry to learn of this latest episode. Please tell Chris that we are thinking of her and praying for her to get over this problem quickly. And, look after yourself Trev. No-

one could be a more loving supporter of Chris than you are, right now. Give our love to Robert and family also.

Gotta go now - we are going to Susan's brother's home for the day. Will Skype you soon.

With love from
Geoff and Susan (Owens)

Hi Trevor,
Pauline and I are very sad to hear that Chris is in hospital, we are thinking of her and hope that she improves soon. Please give her our good wishes for a speedy recovery.

I hope you are coping, please let us know how you both are, when you can.

With all good wishes,
Pauline & Mike xxx (Gibbons)

Trevor,
Our thoughts are with you both. We too hope that she will be able to go home soon.

After such a good year with your trips we hope you managed to have at the least, a bit of a Christmas together.

God bless,
Michael & Sue (Parker)

Just wanted to wish Chris a happy birthday - although I suspect she's had better. Please let her know that we are all thinking of her. Keep strong.

Love
Nick, Sarah, Harry and George (Brown)

Dear Trevor
Never a day goes by without Val and I talking about you two and wondering how Chris is getting on. I've no idea how it could make any difference but we always send you a 'thought wave' and a long-range hug in the hope that it just might help.

We know that Wednesday is a special day in your diary so we'd like to send you a special hug with our love and best wishes on your Anniversary.
Peter & Val (Halman)

Dear Both,

We were so sorry to hear that your Christmas plans had been upset but have been thinking of you both at this time and we are praying for Chris to have the strength to fight on and for Trevor to have the strength to support her at this very testing time.

God bless.

With our love from
Anne & Alan (Pitt) 24th December

I'll Never Get Over You

Over You

~ John Hiatt ~

The weather was truly terrible the whole time Chris was in hospital - This is a photo at Isis I took to show Chris in hospital.

~ I'll Never Get Over You ~

24th December
Are there any 'real' doctors not just these 1st year ward
doctors? It is impossible to get any answers. Bank Holidays.
Weekends. 9 to 5 NHS. I am angry. It doesn't help. The
nurses are great but purely reactive. They don't go to feed
Chris if she doesn't eat. Chris tells me the food is lousy. I
have to leave her. Our first Christmas Eve apart, not at the
pub with our friends as usual. I go to the pub, but it's like
I'm only half there. I am so down.

25th December.
Robert and Pippa arrive lunchtime. Pippa has been brilliantly
supportive to me. Rob and I take Ollie to the hospital where
we are meeting Mum. All the family come up to see her
and Chris manages to open her presents, although we bring
them back home with us. Ollie plays to her a little on his
new guitar but he is embarrassed in front of all the visitors
and other patients. He is upset to see his Granny so ill and
doesn't want to go back in to see her. Chris manages to laugh
with the family but I think we are all upset that we haven't
managed to get her home.

We have to leave her late afternoon to have Christmas. Pippa
does a great job with the dinner but it is not a happy day.
Maybe we are all beginning to realise that this is not getting
better. I don't recall thinking that it was the beginning of the
end, but maybe I did. I cried on Pippa's shoulder that evening,
deep racking sobs of fear and pain. It was my lowest point
of the whole battle. So alone. Chris so brave and alone in
hospital. Thank goodness we have done so much in the year.
It was, I think, the moment I really knew my baby was going
away.

26th December
Back to the hospital. Snow and ice, sub-zero, dire. Chris
really in the best place. No change. No doctors to ask.

Nothing. Chris not eating. I resolve to bring food. I begin
to stay longer every day, sitting with her, holding her hands,
talking, trying to be strong whilst feeling weak. She's the brave
one, uncomfortable but not in great pain, drain still taking fluid
out. So much. Rob and Pip come up later, we're not bringing
Harriet as we think it will upset her too much. Granny
deprived of her greatest love - her grandchildren but we have to
think of their long-term welfare.

27th December
It's Chris's birthday today. She's made it to 60. This was her
target at the beginning when diagnosed. I will make Christmas,
my birthday and our wedding anniversary she told Robert. She
is stubborn! More presents but she is so poorly she can
barely be bothered. She sleeps more each day. The family all
come again. Linda and Robert have been fantastic throughout
the year. Carole also visited and supported regularly, Tony
phoning and having more trouble coping with it all.

28th December
Still a sodding bank holiday! When will I ever get to see
a doctor, a consultant. 9 to 5 NHS. Crap management,
government throwing money but not controlling it. Makes me
sick. Chris is unchanged, still disorientated and anxious. Often
imagining things. We still are putting it down to the drugs. We
have a sad old lady in the next bed, partially suffering from
dementia. She never shuts up! Very off putting and disturbing
for Chris.

29th December
Late afternoon we finally see the chest registrar. We hear
the worst, although I don't think Chris really takes it in or
understands. That morning's scan - taken after I complained
to registrar - shows Chris has a collapsed lung. Also, a
blood clot on right lung. She is too ill to operate. The trauma
would be fatal, but so is the collapse I realise when studying
information on internet. It is the moment that I know she is
in her final days.

Dance Me To The End Of Love

~ Leonard Cohen ~

~ Dance Me To The End Of Love ~

Update 13 – 30th December 2009

Hi,

I trust you had a Happy Christmas, with lots of pressies and fun with the family.

Needless to say my Christmas was very black with Chris in hospital, despite Robert, Pippa, Ollie and Harriet being so kind and supportive around me. Children are amazing creatures, they seem to know instinctively if you are 'wounded'. Ollie and Harriet fussed around me constantly, regularly coming to give me hugs out of the blue, telling me 'I love you' and telling me that Granny would be home soon.

The whole festive season was coloured by establishing that if you are going to be ill and in hospital, be ill Monday to Friday between 9.00am and 5.00pm. On weekends and bank holidays it appears that nothing is working. Can't find a senior doctor to talk to, can't get a CT Scan, can't get an xray, can't get a dietician, can't get a palliative care nurse to review medication, ward nursing just a skeleton staff – over-worked and underpaid. It was a bloody nightmare

Finally, yesterday, my chasing, cajoling and pleading began to show some benefit. In the space of one normal working day (1) palliative pain control team came and changed her pain relief – more later (2) dietician arrived (3) chest consultant spent 25 minutes explaining everything to us – at last (4) she had Chris getting a CT scan in 45 minutes – she'd been waiting SIX days (5) oncologist came to review Chris's case. Action and knowledge at last. It makes dealing with the situation so much less stressful.

Granny is actually pretty poorly. In basic terms we now know she has suffered a collapsed lung. She has been on a lung drain since 7.00pm on Monday 21st. She has been on suction support as well, whilst she is on permanent oxygen to help her breathe. They cannot operate on her because she is too weak and because it is likely her lung is cancerous anyway. We are awaiting test results on the drained fluid. In addition, Chris has a blood clot near/on her left lung which is also receiving treatment by injection..

Her pain relief has proved the most difficult to cope with for me. She can only be described as being 'out of it' since last Monday, eyes shut (not necessarily sleeping) for long periods, or asleep, or when awake simply not really being with it. This has caused me untold worry because it also means that she hasn't been able to look after herself or have a rational conversation with the nurses. It has contributed to her dietary problems because she doesn't want to eat, and unless we were around to push her to eat she didn't bother. She has lost ½ stone in 2 weeks. Bearing in mind she has forced herself to eat during her chemotherapy as part of our survival strategy, it is really disappointing to see this happen in a hospital. They have changed her drugs today so I am hopeful of a return to nearer normality but the changeover takes 48 hrs to completely take affect. There is a humorous side to it, as she regularly suddenly sits up in bed and tells me off or gives me her orders. She briskly told me yesterday that 'we can't afford to go to Antigua', then immediately went back to sleep! Watching her do SuDoko whilst under the influence has also been quite entertaining!

They will be fitting her with a permanent air and fluid lung/chest drain (valve), complete with bag, in next few days and hopefully once that has settled down she will be able to come home. She will not be able to continue her chemotherapy programme, so we await meeting with her oncology consultant to establish a new treatment programme. It is crucial to both of us that Chris has a quality of life, not simply quantity. Dignity is an often misused word, but it has now become very important.

Chris herself is, of course, still in 'I'll be alright' mode because of her natural fighting instincts. How she copes without complaint, assuring everybody that 'I'm alright' continues to astound me. The privilege of loving her has become greater as the year has gone by.

So, my dear friends, we have entered a very difficult period today on our 42nd wedding anniversary. As a family we are beginning to speak of the logistics of looking after Chris when she hopefully returns home in the next couple of weeks and I will be meeting with MacMillan nurses next week. The world has changed for the worse but, as always, we look forward to the new adventure that we are about to face.

Chris and I wish you all a Happy New Year. We hope it will be, above all else, healthy. The wealthy and the wise can come later.

God bless,
Trevor & Chris
xxx

We are so pleased and humbled that you are both 'still in there'. Christmas must have been awful but as you said the children can give you their love and that is such a wonderful thing. Chris has gone on being Chris to the best of her considerable life force and let us pray that this will see her into 2010.

Your updates give us insight into your existence, for that is all it can be at the moment, and your spirit does you proud. Getting to update13 has been amazing so try and make 20.

Please know our thoughts are with you as the Old Year draws to a close
John and Florence (Oliver)

Trevor.
Thank you for the very graphic account of how everything is with you both. You certainly are sharing your lives with us.

We continue to pray for you.

Love and God bless,
Julian (Owens)

Dear Trevor,
Thank you for your sustained news update, and what a Christmas period this has been for you both! You are doing the most amazing and devoted caring for Chris imaginable, and thank God your efforts in hospital eventually paid off. Chris continues to be an inspiration to all with her 'I'll be alright' quips, and her tenacity is an example to all in such bleak circumstances.

God bless you both in the year ahead.

Much love,
Tony and Denise (Wightman)

Hi Trevor,
Thanks for the update. Know what you mean about the 9 - 5 Mon - Fri culture in the NHS.

All I can say is that I am thinking of you. Hope you get Chris home soon.
Steve (Goodman)

Dear Trevor,

Thank you fior the latest on Chris. Our thoughts will be with you during the coming weeks.

With best wishes,
Joyce and Jim

Hello Trevor and Hello Chris,

Thanks once again for keeping us in the picture, I am sure writing out these reports keeps you busy and possibly takes your mind off reality even if just for a few minutes each day. Chris's pluck never ceases to astound Betty and I, and we feel very privileged to have known you both albeit for a very short period of time. Congrats on the wedding anniversary - another milestone gone and the next one to look forward to. Did you say you are booking another cruise? Hope you are, they are great ways of relaxing. We had a lovely Xmas in USA. We missed out on all that snow in the States, we were two states away from Virginia where they got a real hammering. I even played golf 4 times, and prior to that hadn't hit a ball since being in Spain early in November. Mark you, I did manage to jar my wrist so it will be a few weeks before I play again. Physio booked for Monday. We hope you both have a peaceful New Year, and as healthy a one as circumstances will allow.

Love to you both,
Betty & John (Edmundson)

Hi to you both,

Just wanted to say thank you for the continued updates on Aunty Christine. We are all hoping and praying that 2010 sees Aunty Christine back at Isis with you.

All is fine here. All the prep is done for returning to work and school on Monday. We have had a quiet Christmas with no visitors. And with Dean's back problem we couldn't consider travelling north, which was a real shame. Mum and Dad came down in early Dec which was lovely. As soon as Dean has his injection and we see the result, hopefully good, we will be out visiting again.

We are due to move in the summer but as yet don't know where to. Dean may move before that but as I have started a Horticulture course I can't move till July.

Will sign off now as Lewis wants to go to the skate park with his new bike. Fingers crossed we return in an hour with no serious injuries. He is a real dare devil and wants to do tricks!

I hope as I send this that Aunty Christine's meds are working better and that she is more aware of things around her, especially you.

With all our love as always,
Lesley, Dean, James and Lewis xx (Carpenter)

My dear friends,
I am sorry we haven't been in touch as we haven't been home to read the e-mails. You are both going through so much my heart goes out to you both. All we can pray for is Chris doesn't have to suffer too much. The nurses are truly amazing and will help you both so much. Poor Chris is so lucky to have such a wonderful family around her. Richard has been poorly again over Christmas and has been in bed for a week. I had to take him to the hospital today as he has had swine flu and it has turned to a lung infection. I found him over the toilet this morning with the pan full of blood. The doctor was useless and wouldn't even exam him. I have had to look after the pub and Richard but The Runner it is not and I have Simon and Hannah with me to help. Little Jessica has helped too so it has gone quite well. We had an Irish band New Years Eve and over 100 people so everyone had a good time but i feel quite tired as Rich is keeping me awake at night.

Well please give Chris all our love and as ever you are both in our prayers.
Chrissy and Dickie (Probert)

Trevor, take our love to Chris with a hug. Our Cornish family are going through an ordeal with their 15 year old daughter but there may be light at the end of their tunnel. Tamsyn like Chris is a testament to life and both their strengths makes us wonder and gaze on.

Love,
Netty and Julian xxx (Turner)

We wish I had time to call each of you to personally wish you a happy and healthy year, but as most of you know, my son in law Eric has suffered a heart attack at our home in Florida and had quintuple bypass surgery 2 days ago. He is doing as well as can be expected. His family went back to Longmeadow today, to get the girls situated for the next month, and Sharon will be back early in the next week.

Our love to all and hope the new year brings peace, health and well being to all of us.

Love,
Miriam and Albie

Dear Trevor and Chris,

Thanks for your letter and card and your update. Been keeping in touch with you through Aunty Eileen and we've been praying for you at all 4 of my churches. Hope your Christmas was good and that the docs are making sure you get everything possible to get you through this difficult time.

Please keep in touch and here's hoping and praying that 2010 will bring you good news. God bless you both

Much love,
Jane xxx (Facey)

Hi Trevor,
Chris was on both of our minds throughout the Christmas period and very often Chris was mentioned in an everyday, normal conversation.

Your experience with the hospital becoming a 'ghost town' over a weekend is all too true and not just in Wolverhampton. I went through a very similar dilemma exactly 3 months ago with my dear Mum, bless her. It can be extremely frustrating.

Mine and Tina's thoughts and wishes are for Chris, you and of course your family for the New Year

Much love,
Jeff & Tina xx (Hull)

Trevor,
Thank you for your update, I am saddened by the news that Christmas has been so difficult for you all, but am pleased that you were able to hassle and harangue sufficiently to get some progress.

You and Chris and the family will remain in our prayers as ever, and I hope that you are able to get Chris home as soon as is physically (and safely) possible. Congratulations to you both on 42 years together! That is truly a spectacular achievement, especially in the society we live in today!!! J J

Trevor – look after yourselves and keep us posted with how things go. I will make sure we as a church pray for you all again on Sunday.

God bless,
Dave (Tubby)

Trevor & Chris,

We thought of you so much over Christmas and the New Year hoping Chris was with you and your family. By the time you get this we hope she will back in the arms of her family and the Drs have made her as comfortable as possible, it is dreadful to think of her suffering so much.

This time last year you were not expecting to share Xmas 09 with Chris so keep hoping and praying.

Our love and thoughts are with you all.
Pat and Brian (Bourne)

Dear Chris and Trevor,

I would send a video e-mail, but it will be difficult for you to take it with you to the hospital.

We are very grateful that you have kept us in the loop with the tales of Chris's resilience and perseverance and more importantly her positive attitudes that have encouraged many people here in Chile. Today, as a family we have lit candles so that we are reminded of your cause and Chris's fight and battle. A recent family had their son in hospital with a terrible virus on the brain and within three days he was conscious and already on the road to recovery. The most important part of this action is to create a physical force and energy to give to Chris. I'm sorry it's not much but you are in our prayers and thoughts all day and Monica is especially touched by your updates and the power that Chris is showing.

I have a fundamental belief in the attitude and power of positive confession and Chris has shown that by not using negative words, she has overcome many obstacles. I hope you can relay to her the power and influence she has passed to other people on the other side of the world.

We love you both and need you both to continue confessing healing and progress and faith that the doctors are guided to do the best for you both.

Love,
Paul, Monica and Charlotte xxx (Silver)

Trev, please give Chris my love. Let her know that my love and thoughts are with her constantly. I can only imagine how much she must be wishing she could just go home and how u must be feeling not to be able to make everything right. I know u will be doing everything in your power even so. Please give my dear Chris the biggest hug possible for me and remind her how important her friendship is and has been to me over all these years.

Love Deb
xxx (Hanfeld)

Oh I'm sorry Chris can't make it home but yes I'm sure the hospice is the best option for her - she will have 24hr care there. Will you let me know when Chris gets moved then I can visit her at the weekend all being well - if the weather improves! The snow is very bad here 2day and it is still snowing! As always give Chris my love and tell her I will see her very soon

xx Andrea (Stephens)

Thinking of you both.

Much love.
Helen (Leathers)x

Hope ur able to see Chris today. I had hoped to visit today give her my love and will cu soon perhaps at st richards love and prayers Janet (Price)

Hope Chris is comfortable and that u continue 2 have the strength...we apologise 4 never responding but u both are always in our thoughts...hope the weather gives u a break
Tony & Ann (Killoran)

I'm Your Man

~ Leonard Cohen ~

~ I'm Your Man ~

30th December
All is unchanged. Weather is still lousy – snow, ice, sub-zero
and I am taking in food and feeding Chris.

It is only now, reflecting back as I write this with the aid of notes taken, that I realise that I think I knew she was in her last days although I never actually wrote it or said it. My actions were those of a person saying a long goodbye gently. Chris and I never discussed our goodbye at this time, mainly because she really wasn't with it. But we had covered 'goodbye' over the year in different ways and so perhaps we didn't feel the need. I don't know. I share the view with my pal Kim that we were privileged to have the opportunity of saying our long goodbye to the lady in our life because although we fought the battle we always knew what the end result was likely to be. A lot of people don't have the opportunity of a 'long goodbye'.

Our 42nd anniversary was to be our last together, spent holding hands in a hospital and being as much in love as we were on our wedding day. We have been very blessed with happiness and laughter. I have never regretted our life together for one moment, and I don't think Chris did. She once told me (before she was ill) that she had loved her life.

31st December
New Years Eve. Chris unchanged. This was always Chris's night. Not this year. She had a terrible day, not so much in pain but in her disorientation. The afternoon was a nightmare, although she was so far not with it that she didn't realise how bad it was. This day was my lowest day – worse than the night she died. It was simply terrible and I barely coped. The nurses were quite brilliant but it was the day that I knew for certain the game was up.

I saw her oncologist who confirmed by what he didn't say that there was nothing more he could do.

He told me the palliative team would take control of her medication, that it was now important to maintain her dignity and make her comfortable.

1st January 2010

Chris sleeping more as increased drugs take effect. Oxygen helping her but she now has a syringe infusion for her pain relief with a different drug (not morphine). Hopefully this will result in less disorientation.

2nd January

Of course, it's both the weekend and a bank holiday so NHS 9 to 5 applies. The mad woman in the next bed is as bad as ever, and Chris views her with amusement whilst understanding little of the issues. I am there all day from 10.00 every day, bringing her food and feeding her. She has her moments of great clarity (thank goodness) and is aware. We sense a touch of anger within her as she knows she's coming to the end of her quite awesome battle. She has never given in, and even now deep inside is trying to fight to stay with us for eight more days so that her pal Sandra is back from Australia. Her determination is fantastic.

3rd January

I cancel visitors due. Chris is too unwell and they would be too upset. I sit with her, holding hands and talking. Chris sleeps mostly, eats a little when I feed her. It's just a quiet day together (apart from the mad woman next door).

4th January

I'm with her all day again. Mum and Carole visit, with Tara, and for the first time her Mum is distressed. She realises that there is not going to be a miracle cure, the end is close and she can't make her little girl better. She weeps on my shoulder, away from the bed. It is one of the saddest moments of my life. This brave lady, who lost her husband so long ago, who has been the rock of the family in tears as she prepares to lose her daughter. It is unbearable.

I stay with Chris after they've gone. This is a sad day, not a bad day, because Chris is comfortable, dignified and in no pain.

5th January.

I awake to 6' of snow! Sub-zero and a terrible weather forecast. I can't get to the hospital. Robert gets there in his Land Rover, and friends Rowl and Hazel make it across. I take the day off and rest. I'm exhausted.

6th January

Rob has stayed and we go up. When we get there Chris is sitting up, wolfing down her lunch and eating more than she's eaten in the last two weeks! She's not talking. I feed her the last of lunch, she literally eats the lot! Then a porter arrives to take her for a scan! We are surprised but assume it's to check her chest. How wrong were we!

When she returns, over an hour later, she is asleep. She never properly wakes up from this sleep. Late afternoon the palliative doctor arrives to tell us it was a head-scan and Chris appears to have had some sort of stroke.

I now believe this took place the weekend *before* she entered hospital and was the cause of all her disorientation. Who knows? Knowing would have made no difference to her final passing but maybe it would have helped us all understand why she was so disorientated.

We had her moved into a private side-ward that evening.

7th January

When I phoned early morning we were advised to come straight to the hospital. I arranged for all her family to visit today and Pippa came up in the afternoon. Everyone said their goodbyes, and although Chris was 'asleep' she knew they were all there. Pippa woke her to show her photos of Hattie playing in the snow (Chris opened her eyes, looked at them and smiled). Everyone went and I stayed with her for the night.

7th/8th January

I talked to her so much that evening, and even managed a

couple of hours of sleep. I told her I loved her, thanked her for a wonderful life together. I told her that if she was tired of the fight, of the battle, then she should let go and leave me to go and meet her father again. At 3.00am I started to text Sandra in Australia to update her when I noticed Chris's breathing had changed. The nurse came and reassured me, but I felt this was getting very close to her time.

It was difficult to hug Chris, with her drain one side and syringe infusion the other, but I managed to put my arms around her. I then held her close . I kissed her twice, then she very deliberately kissed me back and as I laid her down, holding both her hands, she sighed and she left me for ever.

It was a beautiful way to say goodbye.

As I cried I almost felt her leave her mortal body, I could almost reach out and touch her 'spirit', I could almost feel her looking down at me as I sat holding her hands. But she was gone and the reason for my very being was with me no more.

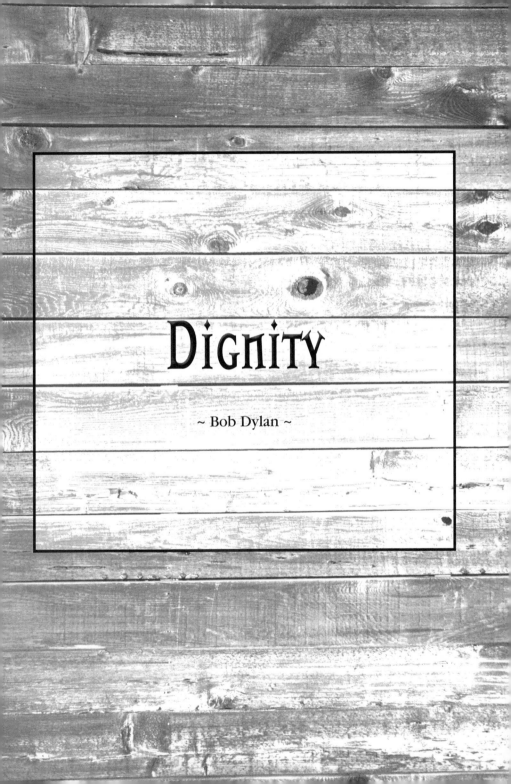

Dignity

~ Bob Dylan ~

A lasting memory. Chris in Corsica. (July 2009)

~ Dignity ~

Update No 14 – 8th January 2010

I'm sorry to tell you that Chris passed away this morning. We will post further details at http://www.girls-have-fun.co.uk/ as things become arranged.

Thank you for all your support.

God bless,
Trevor

I know how terrible all this is. And i know and feel every stage with you. God give you strength. Get some rest Trev when you get home and I will speak with you tomorrow. All my love and prayers are with you.

Love,
Sian x x

She was such a star.
Rowl & Hazel (Charge)

So glad that you were together at the very end Trev. It's so tragic and I offer you all our deepest sympathy. Our love and prayers are with you. Chris's spirit is now happy and free from pain and she will see you again one day in a much better place.

Love,
Sian x x x (Ayckbourn)

Not a good alarm call, but not unexpected. She is at peace with no more pain. How good it was that you were able to be with her at her passing and Robert too I hope. So upset mate.

Bye bye Auntie Christine,
Love D and M xx (Grandison)

My condolences. Let me know if there is anything we can do.

Speak later,
Martin (Davies)

I am working today, but please text when I can speak to you. I know everyone will call and I know how exhausting it will be for you, Robert and the family. Will say prayers for you, Rob and Chris's mum in church tonight, will dedicate the service to Chris. God strength Trev. June leaving us also broke our hearts but the love of family and friends helps you to survive.

Sian x x (Ayckbourn)

Thanks for sending, that must have been the hardest thing. Do you have anyone with you? Shout for anything. Speak soon.
Dave & Kate (Clarke)

So sorry to hear this sad news our thoughts are with you mate.
Roy (James)

Trevor I'm so sorry. Thinking of you all at this very sad time xx
Andrea (Stephens)

Trev. So sorry to hear this news. Pass on our thoughts to all of your family. If u need anything just ask. God bless you and keep Chris safe.
Ian & Chez (Williams)

So sorry to hear about Chris. Our thoughts are with you.

Take care.
Terry (Colley)

A light has gone out in all our lives.

'Courage mon brave.'
Kim (Sharman)

Trev sorry to hear about Chris. All our thoughts are with you and family. If there is anything we can do just let us know.

Regards
Mike (Parker)

Trevor, I am so sorry! I know I didn't get to see Chris but she was always in my thoughts. Chris always made me smile and I still remember the many weekends we spent at yours... I normally fell asleep on the sofa! I know you have a strong back up team to support you but I am always here.

Lindsay (Townend)

Trev,

So very sorry,-our deepest sympathy.Have tried e-mailing a no of times lately but they've bounced back.

Best wishes,
Ken (Lewis)

Sorry to hear your news and that we were unable to visit as we are still away in Bulgaria. The only place around Europe without snow. Will call on our return. Our thoughts are with you.

Love,
Steve, Jackie & Charlie xxx (Hickman)

Our thoughts are with you and the family. The time has gone so quickly and it's still a shock. Her laughter and kindness will be truly missed.

All our love,
Keith & Bev xxx (Windram)

I'm sad to hear Chris has past away she was a lovely lady

Our thoughts are with you and the family. If there is anything we can help with just call.

Lots of love,
Bernie & Billy x (McLaughlin)

Trev, so very sorry! Our thoughts are with u all. Just call if u need anything. xx
Terry & Carole (Allsop)

Hi Trev, I have just heard of your sad news. Chris fought so bravely through 2009 to make Xmas and her 60th birthday. A true inspiration to us all. Our thoughts are with you.

God bless.
Paul and Sue x (Blake)

Sorry to hear the news Trevor my thoughts to you and family
Doug (Howard)

You will be busy and feeling fragile and needing time but if there is anything i can do please say.

Take care, love,
Janet (Price)

Hi Trev, We' re here quietly knowing the pain you and the family must feel at this moment. We will miss the endearing, caring, courageous human being she was.

God bless all of you at this time.
Ian and Cherry. Xx (Williams)

There's a bed here if you need some comfort and support. Chez and me are here if you need support when your family go back to do what they have to do over the next few days.

God bless.
Ian & Chez xx (Williams)

Such a sad day! So many fond memories of Chris. Speak to you soon.

Love,
Ann & Bill (Beard)

Dear Trevor, my heart goes out to you as I recall Hil's last stay in the hospital in Austria. In those 10 days I was closer to her then ever but that's not to say it didn't break my heart and yes dignity and a 'good death' is all. My thoughts and prayers are with you all.

Clare (Farrands)

Bless you. Thinking of you. Take care speak soon.

With love from all of us.
Ewout, Hayley, Willem and Anjes (van der Kleijn)

Dear Trevor,
I'm so sorry to hear about Chris, she was such a fighter, you were blessed with so much extra time with her than you first thought. God bless - my thoughts and prayers are with you and your family.

Best wishes,
Alison (Holmes)

Dear Trevor,
I am so sorry to hear your news.

I think that the way in which Chris dealt with her illness and the way in which you supported her was truly remarkable.

You are both in our prayers.
Robert (Geary)

Trevor, how can we ever tell you how saddened we are to hear about Chris. We only knew her for two short weeks, but she was the pluckiest person I've ever come across and your loss must be shattering. You are in our thoughts and prayers.

Betty & John.(Edmundson)

Trevor,
So very sorry to hear this news.

Thinking of you and hoping that you will be able to focus on the good memories of which you must have so many.

Tony (Ericson)

Joyce and I were very saddened to hear about Chris and send you our deepest sympathy. She has been a wonderful example of courage during this dreadful ordeal and you must be very proud.

With all our thoughts,
Jim (Williams)

Trevor,
Very sorry to hear your news, our sympathies to you and your family for your sad loss. We are thinking of you.

Steve (Goodman) & Tony (Ericson)

Hi Trevor,
Karen and I are so sorry to hear about Chris. She was a role model of making sure that you live life to the full irrespective of the cards that are dealt to you. We also have huge admiration for you and the way that you have helped and supported through her illness.

The memories and the life and love that you shared together will always be with you. Our thoughts are with you and your family at this time. Take care my friend

Kind regards,
John (Frost)

Trevor,

My deepest sympathies. If there is any thing at all that I or Fiona can do please let me know.

Thinking of you,
Paul (Bradford)

Dear Trevor,
Every wish of sympathy for you and the family.

Clare and Paul.

Dear Trevor,
It has been a difficult road for you and you must be totally exhausted and upset. Now is not the time for trite words. We are thinking of you and remembering a lovely person and the good times.

John & Florence (Oliver)

Dear Trevor,
My thoughts and prayers are with you and Chris, God rest her soul.

Stephen (Barclay)

Sorry to hear that dear Chris passed away this morning. I thank God that you were able to be with her. I pray for your peace and comfort in the Lord and in knowing that you did all, and more, that you could have done for her. God bless.

Janet (Price)

Trevor,
I am so sorry, my condolences please.

Take care,
Janet (Peacock)

Dear Trev,
So sorry to hear of Chris's passing, glad you were with her to comfort her at the end. We will always remember her cheerful courage, this time we are sure she will reach the light.

Love,
Brian and Steph (Delmas)

Trevor,

Our sincere condolences to you and your family, our thoughts and prayers are with you all. You and everyone else will cherish so many wonderful memories of Chris.

Love,
Pat and Brian (Bourne)

Hi Trevor,

So very sad - my heart goes out to you. It has been a very sad week as my Nan passed away a week ago today. I'm thinking of you and Robert and his family and send you a poem that I find really helps (you may have already heard it). Love, hugs and best wishes.

Chrisy xx (Cross)

Death is nothing at all,
I have only slipped into the next room
I am I and you are you
Whatever we were to each other, that we are still.
Call me by my old familiar name,
Speak to me in the easy way which you always used
Put no difference in your tone,
Wear no forced air of solemnity or sorrow
Laugh as we always laughed at the little jokes we enjoyed together.
Play, smile, think of me, pray for me.
Let my name be ever the household word that it always was,
Let it be spoken without effect, without the trace of shadow on it.
Life means all that it ever meant.
It it the same as it ever was, there is unbroken continuity.
Why should I be out of mind because I am out of sight?
I am waiting for you, for an interval, somewhere very near,
Just around the corner.
All is well.

Henry Scott Holland

1847-1918

Canon of St Paul's Cathedral

Trevor,

Sue and I are very sorry to hear of Chris's passing. I was talking to Geoff this morning and he relayed to me how you felt you and Chris had had a miracle year.

Based on what you have said about Chris I think part of that miracle was that she was given the opportunity to find peace with God. When people are taken suddenly they don't get that chance.

Being at peace with God, knowing her sins are forgiven means that she has now passed from death to life. She is now in eternity with Christ. This is not because of her goodness but because of His perfect love demonstrated to us by his death on the cross followed by bodily resurrection. That is the Christian hope that as a believer, Chris will share in.

You may not have the time or inclination to read many emails at the present time but in case you do, I would like to say one more thing.

I guess you must be facing a dark and uncertain future. Just a few days ago at New Year, I was reminded of the speech given by King George VI at the end of 1939 when Britain was facing an uncertain future. He included the following poem in his speech:

'I said to the man who stood at the gate of the year, "Give me a light that I may tread safely into the darkness".

He replied "Put your hand into the hand of God and you will find this to be brighter than a light and safer than a known way".'

God bless you Trevor.

Love and God bless,
Julian (Owens)

Trev ... sad, sad news indeed. Chris is now out of pain and at rest. God bless her and you. ..... John and Jill)Caruth)

Dear Trevor,

My name is Kris and I don't know if you will remember me, but you employed me to run with the office products at EMTEC back in 2001.

I have just heard the terrible news about Chris and I just wanted to say that my thoughts are with you and your family at this difficult time.

I hope our paths cross again because it would be lovely to see you. Working for you at EMTEC was the best job I ever had. I am just starting to build my own business and I'm trying to create the same 'family' culture you created at EMTEC.

If ever you fancy a chat, glass or two of Jameson single malt whisky (I think that was your tipple) or a game of golf please get in contact.

Kindest regards,
Kris (Taylor)

So sorry to hear that Trevor. We have been remembering you both in our prayers and will continue to ask for peace for you.

Love,
Dave & Di Morgan

Trevor, our hearts go out to you and your family. It was our privilege to have known her.

Love,
Albie and Miriam

Trev,
I'm ever so sorry to hear this and am thinking of you.

I'm conscious that I haven't been very communicative these last few

months and owe you an explanation, which I'll give in due course.

Suffice for now to say that things here are not good. More another time.

With love from us all
S, B, H, & A (Shepherd)

Dear Trevor,
I am so sorry – words cannot express how sad Carol and I feel. Our thoughts are with you and the family at this very difficult time.

Regards,
Gary & Carol (Milner)

Hello Trev,
Thank you for letting me know.

Look after yourself, Trev - that is the important thing now. Chris is at peace - and you know that you did as much as any person could to ensure that she was comfortable and at peace - and she knows it too!

Faith is a tough thing to get to grips with - so hang on tight during this time of difficulty.

Please let me know what the arrangements are likely to be - I might be able to get there -not sure yet-so I need good notice.

We love you,
Geoff (Owens)

Oh Trevor,
I am so so sorry – I know you both had a very long and brave battle against all odds – You have all my sympathy – I am so sorry

Shirl (Hunter)

Hello Trevor,
Dave and Yvonne here, just read your extremely sad email.

It is at times such as this where words can never express the sadness that is felt, nor in a peculiar sort of way the joy of having known them.

We can all roll out the usual clichés but sometimes it is better to just remember and on that note let us leave you with one thought told to us by a neighbour from Valley View.

'As long as they are in your mind and heart they are alive, all that has happened is they stop making memories.'

God bless you all.
Dave and Yvonne (Genner)

I am sorry to hear about Chris falling asleep. She is at peace and out of pain .

Clive (Fowler)

Dear Trevor,
I am so very sorry to hear the sad news. It is almost impossible to write any words that can console you in your loss. As you know I only met Chris a couple of times but all I can say her past years journey has shown her to be a truly remarkable person. As I have said before the courage, strength and resilience you both showed in the past year made me very humble. My thoughts are with you and the family.

God bless,
Keith (Fleming)

Hi Trevor,

So sorry to hear about your loss and even though she battled against this dreadful disease fantastically - it is still a shock to hear she is no longer with us. She was a wonderful lady and we are both happy and grateful to have known her in the relatively short time we have been friends.

Hopefully see you soon.

With deepest sympathies,
Marc, Sarah & Samantha (Staniszewski) xx

Hi Trevor,
So sorry to hear the news, our thoughts and love are with you and your families.

So glad that you and Chris had a year to remember and that you reached Christmas, your anniversary and Chris's birthday even if not quite as you had hoped. I have just spoken to Sue and I understand that you were with her overnight and that all the families had been with her yesterday as well.

Will keep watching for the arrangements and hopefully all the snow will disappear soon.

Lots of love,
Rob & Judy (Price)

Hello Trevor,
I just wanted to let you know I am thinking of you at this sad time.

With all my love,
Andrea (Searle)

Hi Trevor,
I'm so sorry to receive your news, I was thinking about you both all day yesterday and was going to ring tonight. My thoughts and prayers and my love are with you all.

With fond memories of Chris and prayers for strength for you as cope with all the arrangements that you have to make.

Love,
Jane (Facey) xxx

Dear Trevor,

Even though I've not responded to them, I've read all of your updates with humble admiration of you both. It's impossible to put into words what you must be feeling, so I'll simply say that I feel some fraction of your sadness with you.

You're in our thoughts and prayers.

God bless,
Jem and Eva (Shaw)

Dear Trevor,

Pauline and I are deeply saddened by your news today. Although we only knew you and Chris for a very short time, we felt like you were lifelong friends.

I cannot put into words, how we feel at this moment. Although we knew Chris was very ill, it is still a great shock.

I will be in touch again soon.

With deepest sympathy,
Mike & Pauline (Gibbons)

Trevor,

I'm so sorry to hear this. We will continue to pray for you at church. You remain in our prayers at this difficult time.

God bless,
Dave (Tubby)

Hope you are coping, sorry will not be able to come to funeral as I am going to be in Australia till Feb, hope everything goes well.

Andy (Harris)

Trevor,

Very sorry to hear your very sad news. I have admired your fortitude and courage through your many updates and Chris's fighting spirit. I cannot start to imagine what it is like to see your life partner suffer so much and lose the final battle. Our heartfelt condolences. We shall be thinking of you.

All our love,
Richard & Jan (Price)

Dear Trevor,

So very, very, sorry. Our thoughts and prayers are with you.

Nigel and Mary (Dunand)

Dear Trevor,

I was so sorry to hear of your sad news today. I'm sure Chris was a very brave, loving and courageous lady who will be sadly missed.

Take care, be strong and stay safe.

Sincerely,

Graham (Perry)

Dear Trevor,

I am so sorry to hear the news but so pleased she was at peace with you. She will know how much you cared. Remember all the good times and rejoice in your family.

Take care,

Sue (Ballard) - Pancreatic Cancer UK

Hi Trevor,

So sorry to hear of your loss.

Best wishes,

Julie (Owen)

Dear Trevor,

I know it's been a while since we've spoken and I'm so sorry that doing so is under these circumstances. My deepest sympathy, Trevor, to you and your family.

Kind regards,

Peter (Lambie)

Sorry to hear your sad news, my thoughts are with you and your family .No words can express the sorrow you are feeling. I am sure that the wonderful memories of your life together will help you in the darkness.

Best wishes

Duncan (Smith)

Trevor,

Our prayers are with you.

Tony (McDowell)

Dear Trevor,

Thank you for letting me know your sad news. This is the time to draw down on the good memories.

Both my mother and grandmother suffered from pancreatic cancer … so I am aware of the scenario you have been supporting over the past months.

My thoughts are with you at this time

Regards,
Chris (Wright)

PS We have just moved to Bridgnorth and finally hung up our 'working boots'.

Dear Trevor,

I am very sorry to hear your sad news. Please accept my condolences. My thoughts and prayers are with you and your family at this time.

Blessings,
Helen (Guinness)

Dear Trevor,

I am so sorry to hear your news.

From what I have read, I am sure that Chris, although in transition, will always be at your side.

Love,
Stephen (Charlton)

Dear Trevor,

So sorry to read your sad news.

My sincere condolences to all your family and friends. Thank you for letting me know.

Sincerest regards,
Chris (Wall)

Trev we are all saddened by your news. All we can do is send you our condolences and let you know we are thinking about you and you are in our prayers. May your many wonderful memories give you comfort in the days to come and ease your pain, Chris will be greatly missed.

Heather and Mark, Sammie, Alex and Craig (Tomlinson)

Hi Trevor,
I'm so sorry to hear about Chris. Just a quick email to let you know that I'm thinking of you and your family at this time.

Helen (Dowling)

Dear Trevor,
Both Claire and I were very sad to hear your news. Although I met Chris only very briefly during my time at Emtec, it was clear that she was a lovely, vibrant person, and I'm sure you will miss her greatly.

Please accept our sincere condolences. We will be thinking of you.

All the best,
Andrew (Watts)

Dear Trevor,
Sean and I are both saddened by this news.

We can only imagine the deep sadness you must be feeling right now but you have a wonderful family and friends around you for love and support and who need you.

I know Chris is no longer with you in body but there must be many wonderful memories for you to look back on so she will always be with you in heart and mind.

Liz and Sean (Forde) xx

Dear Trevor - I am so sorry to hear your news and my thoughts are with you all.

Take care.
John (Hepworth)

My dear Trevor,
My heartfelt condolences to you and your family at this time.

I will keep an eye on the link to follow arrangements.

God bless Chris and may He keep His arm firmly around you.

Tony (Wightman)

Trevor,
So sorry to hear the news. Hope you're coping best you can. Keep in touch.

Take care,
John/Jean (Robinson)

Trevor,
Our thoughts are with you at this time.

We are thinking of you. Keep strong.

Tim & Sharon (Woolridge)

Beverley Gail Manning commented on your status.

'I'm so sorry to hear about Chris, thank you so much for always keeping me up to date with her situation. Please send my condolences to Trevor and her family, I always remember her as being a lovey lady, met her in 1980 at your place. You look after yourselves, it is a sad time for all. We have Sandy's funeral today. Lots of love.'

Hi Trevor,
Very sorry to hear your sad news.

Take care,
Martin(Lyness)

Trevor,
I am very sorry to hear your news. All I can say is that a lot of people are praying and thinking of Chris and you and your family.

God bless you in this difficult time,
Peter (Westbrook)

Hi Trevor,
Sorry to hear the news of Chris passing on, my thoughts are with you and your family at this difficult time.

Take care, God bless,
Matt (Bruton)

Trevor, our thoughts are with you at this difficult time.

All the best,
Peter and Margaret (Spalton)

Dear Trevor,
Your sad news at the end of last week has left me struggling with what to say. Sorry says so little or so much - in my case it just begins to show my deep regret for your loss. As you know I'm not short of experience of bereavement that isn't supposed to happen - Chris should have been with you for another 20 years. But the single overwhelming thing that came out of all of your updates was the joy that you had while you were together - bank that joy and use it in moments that will be only too frequent when life looks so much less enjoyable.

Chris was obviously very strong and very brave over the last year or so. Don't forget that you were too and your strength will have been added oxygen for Chris's fighting flame. Keep your strength alive and show Chris your continuing determination to look after yourself, your children and your grandchildren.

Hoping to be in touch soon.

With sympathy and fondest regards,
Tony (Mills)

Dear Trevor,
My thoughts are with you.

God bless,
Nigel (Clegg)

Very sorry to hear this Trevor.

My sincere condolences, thoughts and prayers are with you.

John (Cave)

Trev, I'm so sorry. Prob. With phone, only got text 2 day. I feel heartbroken. Pete look 4 website. My prayers with you. Understand how u feel. Luv AnneX (Baker)

Dear Trevor,
I have just read the email regarding Chris.

This is a particularly sad time and Kirsty joins me in offering you our deepest condolences at this time.

Kindest regards,
John (Cripps)

Dear Trevor,
I am so very sorry to hear of your sad news, my thoughts are with you at this very difficult time.

When you feel up to it, please give me a call so that we can arrange to meet up. The best number to reach me on is xxx.

Kind regards,
Torben (Jensen)

Hello and good afternoon Trevor,
I am terribly sorry to hear about your lovely wife Chris. I have never written an email message like this before but without your home address I am unable to make it more personal. I think that although I found some of your writing almost too painful to read, what came over was that you had a fabulous last year with both family and close friends. I guess when you compare that with all the people that lose loved ones in a split second, there is something small to be thankful for.

All the very best to you for now Trevor, and for the future.
Tim (Kidson)

Dear Trevor,
I am so sorry for your loss. I'll be thinking of you.

Many best wishes,
Nick (Usansky)

Dear Trevor,
I am very sorry to read your sad news. Please accept my sincere condolences for you and your family at this difficult time.

With kindest regards,
Paul (Werth)

@@@@ (hugs) from Mike & Penny (Gordon) XXXX

Dear Trevor,

I am sorry to hear the news about Chris, please except our condolences.

Regards,
Jayesh (Mianger)

Dear Trevor,

Words fail us all at time like this and I cannot begin to imagine to understand what you have been through in recent months. However, for what it's worth, since you broke the news about Chris's illness you have not been far from our thoughts and we did, as always, offer prayers for you and your family this weekend at mass.

I have forwarded your email on to both Louise and Adrian [Grainger] as I have spoken to Lou today and saw Adrian this morning.

Louise and myself are both planning to be at the funeral to support you as much as we can.

Kind regards,
Chris (Hallett)

Alison (Cheyne) commented on your wall post:

'Thinking of you, sorry to hear this sad sad news xxx'

Dear Trevor and family,

I am so sorry for your loss. But am so glad that you had some time with Chris that you didn't initially think you had, creating some new memories and spending time with each other. I am sure that will be a blessing to you now and in the weeks to come. I just wanted to let you know that I am thinking of you.

With lots of love,
Helen (Leathers)

Hi Trevor,

Never quite sure what to say at such times apart from my deepest sympathies. Although it's not so long since I lost my mother to cancer, I guess that it's nothing like losing a lifelong partner and soulmate. I'm sure that with the support of family and your wide circle of friends you will somehow cope.

Take care.
Adam (Archer)

Trevor - what can I say? So sorry to hear your news. We went through Elizabeth having the big C and both boobs off a decade ago and this summer both her sisters had the same. That said my thoughts will be with you.

God bless,
Tony (Taylor)

Dear Trevor,
On behalf of all of us at Griffiths & Pegg, can I send our deepest condolences to you and your family at this sad time.

I hope to see you again soon.

Regards,
Adrian (Grainger)

Thank you for keeping me informed. What a lovely website you have done for Chris.

Glynis (Ash)

Dear Trevor,
Marilyn and I want to send our love to you, Robert and the family, and also unfortunately to give our apologies for not being able to attend on 25th.

We are booked to stay with 3 other couples in Chipping Camden on Sunday and Monday nights.

Nevertheless you all continue to be in our thoughts and prayers.

God bless you and the family.
Dave & Marilyn (Dippie)

Trevor, my sincere and heartfelt sympathy.

Jonathan (Davies)

Hi Trev,
We were very sad to hear that Chris's fight was now over. You have our deepest sympathy at the end of what must have been a very difficult time for you both. I know I couldn't have coped as you both did.

I was thinking the other day that I must have known Chris since 1960 when we were both in Mr Penny's class at Stanley Road School - almost 50 years.

Geoff is hoping to get a flight and come to the funeral so we will probably come together. At least one of us can then have a drink to Chris's memory.

Our sincerest condolence to you, Robert and the family.
Andy & Wendy (Owens)

Dear Trevor,
I don't know what to say apart from we both have had a terrible time and I am so sad to hear about Chris.

We must try to keep in touch. I have recently met someone and am now living with her about 20 minutes from Tetbury. I found life without Penny very difficult and am very lucky in this totally unexpected luck.

I am off skiing with Claudia and will be in touch on return. It was on the 23 Jan when Penny died so January not a good month.

All my very best wishes and try to remain like the old Trevor!!

yrs,
Tom (Panton)

Dear Trevor,
Very sorry to hear the news. My every sympathy for your loss

Best wishes,
David (Kelham)

Sorry will be not able to come as in Aus. There is not anything I can say I think that can help you through the day only to think of all the happies you and Chris have had through your live together.

Regards,
Andy (Harris)

Trevor,
I was very sad to hear of your loss. My thoughts are with you.

Best wishes,
Bill (Merry)

Hi Trevor
My home phone number is xxx. Spoke to Linda who was at Aunty Eileen's. I'm so

glad the family had the opportunity to say their goodbyes and that you were able to be with Chris right through. We will be praying for you all in my churches today and for as long as you need us to.

With love,
Jane (Facey)

Hello Trev,
I will be there on the 25th. I am arriving in UK on Thursday Jan 21st. Alan is picking me up from Heathrow. Taking a train to Solihull on Friday afternoon to stay with Gemma. Going to stay at Andy's on Sunday night. He will come to the funeral with me. Tuesday morning, Andy will drive me to Heathrow.

See you there. Take care of yourself.

Geoff (Owens)

Dear Trevor,
Peter and I were very sorry to hear of Chris's passing. Our thoughts and prayers are with you and your family.

God bless,
Bryonie (Harwood)

Dear Trev,
So sorry to hear that Christine has finally left us, but at least the suffering for her has ended. You must be exhausted after your long haul. Taking care of her every need day after day in the exemplary way you have can only be mentally and physically draining, but at least you have had the rewards of Christine remaining with you longer than expected.

You are in our thoughts mate.
Chris and Carolyn (Sturges)

Trevor,
Really sorry to hear this news – and you have my deepest sympathies. We only met the once I think when we bumped into you both on the cross channel ferry a few years ago. It must have been very difficult times for you recently – and I hope the emphasis on celebration at the funeral and after means you can go through this on a positive note and concentrate on the many happy memories.

With very best wishes and I'll be thinking of you on the 25th.

Andrew (Cross)

Trevor,

It's been a long long time since our paths have crossed. Firstly, both Win and I would like to convey our sincere condolences to both you and your family on the very sad loss of Chris. We both have wonderful and still vivid memories of you both going back all those years – not only supporting the City – which for my troubles I still do – but also the folk nights at the Perdiswell and Old Bush etc. Still occasionally bump into the likes of Tim Phillips, Rod Harris, Rod Shone –what great times we all had! All the very very best to you Trevor and if you would like to meet-up sometime in the future, please get in touch.

Our very best regards Trevor,

Tony & Win (Speer)

Dear Trevor,

I've just read the sad news about Chris. I used to spend a lot of time on different PC discussion boards but don't go on as much now but I was really touched by your posts and of course so upset to read the sad news about Chris. I've had a look at the farewell web page and it reduced me to tears but all I can say is I'm glad you did have that extra time and were able to do so many things together. Chris reminded me of my own Mum who has now been fighting this nasty disease for 4 years. We were originally told Mum had about 6 months but after a second opinion Mum was lucky enough to have whipple surgery. We have been so lucky to have had this extra time and like you we have used it to go on many trips and do lots of things together.

Anyway Trevor I just wanted to say sorry to read about Chris but well done to you for being such a wonderful carer and advocate for her. This disease is so hard and touches so many lives. I hope one day they will find a cure and better treatment.

Take care,

Claire (Slater-Mamlouk) (via Pancreatic Cancer UK)

Hi Claire

Thank you for your kind letter. I have found the Pancreatic Cancer UK forum very supportive over the months. We considered that Chris was 'living a miracle' in the time we had last year. We were told such a short time initially but thanks to all the prayers, support, positive thinking, distance healing etc etc combined with Chris's steely determination not to give in she achieved her twelve months.

We set ourselves targets all the time by booking holidays nearly every month, and working them into her chemo programme. She had 21 treatments in all, but through them all she continued to eat and refused to accept that she should not go out to lunch, or not visit friends etc. She was truly amazing.

We'll be posting the Church tributes on the website on Monday (maybe the Order of Service as well) if you should want to read them.

Thanks once again. I hope your Mum continues to defy the odds.
Trevor

Dear Trevor,
I was terribly sorry to hear about Chris. Apologies for not responding sooner but I rarely use this hotmail account these days.

Trevor, please accept my sincere condolences. These past few years must have been particularly draining for you on an emotional level. I'm sure Chris would pay tribute to you as a soul mate and truly appreciated your love and support through out her illness.

Sincere best wishes,
Paul (Johnston)

Dear Trevor,
What can I say except that my thoughts are with you and your family at this sad time.

I also lost my Dad on the 12th of December but he was 88 years of age and, I must say, he had a very good life!!

Trevor, you must have so many happy memories and I am sure that these will help you to appreciate the time that you and Chris shared.

Sending you a big hug and I do hope that you know you have friends in Cala who would love to see you again soon.

Take care,
Lynda (Walsh Furlong), Directora, Hotel Cala Sant Vicenç

Dear Trevor,
I am so glad that you were able to have your miracle 12 months and to do so many

things in the time you had. Your wife was an amazing woman and an inspiration to so many. I have read many of your posts and they really touched me. I'm sorry that this disease finally caught up with her but you know she fought as hard and for as long as she could. So sorry you couldn't have had longer together but treasure all those happy memories. As I said she does remind me a lot of my Mum. She is also such a fighter and we too have fitted in as many trips and events over the last four years in between treatments. Mum went for chemo the other day and I know she was telling them she needed to fit in her summer holidays! She is also always out going for lunch and seeing friends. Thank God for our own miracle here. Mum was initially only given 6 months but then we found a surgeon able to do surgery. We are still fighting the recurrence but you really wouldn't know it to see the energy Mum has. I just wish more people could be diagnosed earlier and that surgery could be an option for more people. I would be very interested to read all the tributes to Chris but I have to admit that just seeing her photos and reading what I did online reduced me to tears last time.

Take care of yourself Trevor.
Best wishes,

Claire (Slater-Mamlouk) (via Pancreatic Cancer UK)

I am very sorry to hear your sad news. My thoughts are with you and your family.

All my love,
Kathy Astley xx

Dear Trevor,
I found out at the weekend about the tragic death of Chris. Words can't express the sadness that you must feel at this time. I hope that slowly this sad time passes eventually, and is replaced with happy fond memories. Obviously I have not seen you and Chris for a while, but I do remember her back in the BASF days. I clearly remember her strength and dignity when she battled with a brain haemorrhage back then. She was clearly a wonderful strong woman who will be desperately missed by many for a long time.

I wish you all the best over the coming months, and hope that are able to come to terms with this tragic loss.

Best wishes,
Rob Cooper

Chris was always a pleasure to see and had a fantastic attitude and was always positive in her outlook. You supported and cared for her wonderfully and I know she will be greatly missed.

Glynis (Ash) - MacMillan

Trevor,
Thinking of you and your family at this very sad time.

Love,
Geoff, Sue (Townsend) & family, John, Wendy (Kite) & family, Pam (Lock) & family.

CONDOLENCE BOOK on www.girls-have-fun.co.uk

Dean Carpenter

I'm sorry to you all for your loss. What a fighter. You can all be extremely proud of Chris. Love & blessings are with you.

Mandy Cottle

So sorry to hear Chris has passed away, she gave a good fight & you should all be proud. Thoughts, love and blessings are with you all x

John & Florence (Oliver)

We were privileged to know Chris and know she tried so hard.

Janet & Richard Peacock

Chris gave a good fight and now she is at peace, our thoughts and prayers are with you all. Take care.

Anne & Alan Pitt

Life is too short when you love someone so much. May God take care of you and your family and give you the strength to carry you through the following days, weeks, months and indeed the future. We are so sorry and saddened at the great loss of Chris, we will always remember her and will be thinking of you and send you all our love.

Lesley Carpenter

Uncle Trevor, Robert & family. I am so sorry to hear of your loss. Aunty Christine was so brave, she will be greatly missed by all who knew her. The fight she put up is an inspiration to us all, with much love as always. xx

Cathy & Jared Pogmore

So sorry to hear of Chris's passing. Our thoughts and prayers go out to you and your family. God Bless xx

Kim Sharman

This is a sorrow shared as my Susie passed away last October. Trevor, you and I have given each other such support and comfort that a deeper friendship has come out of it. A small positive out if it all.

She looked terrific, and you have been left a treasure chest of memories. And you had the miracle of much more time together than you could have ever wished for. We'll meet soon. Kim.

Barry, Carol & Pippa

Trevor, Robert and family. Words cannot express our sadness at the loss of our dear friend Chris.

We cherish the memory of times together. To live in hearts we leave behind is not to die at all. Love to you all.

Dave & Marilyn

God Bless you and the family Trevor.

Marilyn and I want you to know that you all continue to be in our thoughts and prayers.

Chris is now at peace in a better place, and the precious times you had together will always remain with you. Love to you all.

Jem Shaw

It's been a humbling and uplifting experience to see and admire the way you both approached this vast mountain. God bless you both.

Wendy Carr

Our thoughts and prayers are with you. You will be sadly missed, rest in peace Chris - gone but not forgotten.

Betty & John

We only knew Chris for two short weeks last summer. She was inspiration to all, especially those who suffer that awful disease, and Trevor - please look after yourself now. All our love, Betty & John,

Sian & Mike Ayckbourn

It was a pleasure to know Chris, such a fun, warm and loving lady. We will miss her dearly, but will always keep her in our hearts and prayers. Chris's spirit is all around us and will continue to inspire us in our daily lives. Our deepest sympathy to you Trev, Rob, Pippa, Ollie, Harriet & Chris's Mum. Love from Sian, Mike and family xx.

Juliana

A hard and valiant fight was fought by you both. All my love to you and your family Trevor, stay strong and support each other. x

Catherine Allan

Chris, you will be greatly missed by all your family and friends, you always gave great advice for all those willing to listen. I was one and will always follow your advice to stay young.

Thank you for a being a wonderful aunt and friend.

Heather & Mark Allan
Chris you were a great aunt. I always thought of you and Trev as my 'cool' aunt and uncle, you both lived life to the fullest and inspired me to do the same although you may not have realised it. Chris you have been an inspiration to many, in the last year especially, and you will be greatly missed. God bless you.

Blind Lemon
We're all very sad to hear the news. Chris was a very special lady. Our thoughts and blessings are with you Trev and your family.

Netty & Julian
Trev and family. We are saddened by the news of this special person who touched all who met her. But fun memories will ever fade; a special person who has brought us inspiration.

We are both out in Pflugerville Texas where Ashley emigrated and got married yesterday; both he and Haley send their love and prayers. love Netty & Julian x

Gary & Deborah
Gary & I cannot express enough how sorry we are to hear that Chris has passed. Words are never enough, so please accept our very deepest sympathy.

Please know that our prayers and thoughts are with you and the family during this most difficult time. With love and sorrow, Gary & Debbie Murrish

Tony W
Dear Trevor. You have both given us such a lesson in wisdom in dealing with the terrible illness Chris has had to endure. Inevitably the end has come, but it is no less devastating when it does.

God bless you both and may Chris rest in peace. With heartfelt condolences, Tony.

Paul & Sue
A very tough 2009 with many highs and lows but full of inspiration from someone who showed incredible courage and determination. A lesson for us all with an incredible never say die attitude.

God bless, all our love Trevor and stay strong. Paul & Sue x

Tim & Sharon
We were saddened to learn of Chris's passing. We knew her for such a short-time when compared with the length of time her network of friends have known her.

For us she was a down to earth, no nonsense lass who we felt we had known for many years on our first time meeting - such was her warmth.

The words from the reading 'All is Well' spring to mind and having read them today it would certainly seem fitting to Chris.

God bless, sending Trevor & the family our love.

David & Marie
Over 40 years of past memories dear friend! You left us too early Chris. But what a brave lady you were over your last months with us! Truly amazing!

Trev, your strength as you looked after your dear wife was also a lesson for us all!

2009 will be the worst year in your lives, but boy did you pack in some great times for Chris as well!

'May God bless and always keep you, may you stay forever young' xx

Val & Peter
As a teenager Chris was bright-eyed, full of fun, usually unimpressed by authority and unfailingly generous of spirit. How wonderful it was that she never changed.

Trevor, we have been deeply moved by the way that you and Chris faced the situation with such fortitude and imagination. Chris's bravery in the face of her illness makes us feel humble. We are greatly saddened at her loss and will now have to rely on the rich store of happy memories of such a lovely person and very dear friend.

With our love to you and all the family. Val & Peter

Peter Spalton
Trevor, our thoughts are with you at this difficult time. God bless, Peter & Margaret

Doug Howard
Thoughts are with you and family Trevor

Tim & Vicki

Trev, we are very sad to hear that Chris's fight is over, but have taken great heart from the manner and way that you both handled the whole battle.

And we will always have those fond memories from both here in Australia & in the UK - something we can keep forever. God bless.

Jeff & Tina

Trevor, we both felt a deep sadness when we learnt of Chris's passing. Our thoughts go out to you and your family.

Ian Fletcher-Price

Dad, myself, Jack & Holly were really sorry to hear your sad news. However, we have all been inspired by your amazing Newsletters that demonstrated such hope and spirit. I have read them to the children to show them how one can be positive in the face of adversity. Our thoughts are with you, Ian.

Gary & Carol

We are so sorry to learn your sad news. We are thinking of you and your family at this difficult time. With sympathy, Gary & Carol xxx

Shirley Hunter

My thoughts and prayers are with you Trevor and your family during this time. I know CHris put up a gallant fight against over-whelmimg odds - I am just so sorry - you must miss her terribly. Shirley

Roy & Carol James

'Life is not a journey to the grave with the intention of arriving safely in a pretty and well preserved body, but rather to skid in broadside, thoroughly used up, totally worn out, and loudly proclaiming -WOW - What a Ride!'

Edward & Hayley van der Kleijn

Having known you & Chris only a short time, we want to thank you for your kindness and wisdom and for sharing your journey over the past couple of years. It has been inspiring and we really enjoyed meeting Chris and your family at the party in the rain. Best wishes, Edward & Hayley.

Ann & Bill Beard

Dear Trevor, Robert & family

Thinking of you all at this very sad time but know that you will show the courage and dignity that has been so obvious throughout the last year. I'm sure Chris will be dealing with this in her usual way that we all knew and loved. God Bless.

Carole & Terry
How can you thank someone for 30 years of friendship in a short message and tell them what it has meant to you? You can't.

We just want to say simply 'Thank You Chris'. It has been our privilege and pleasure to know you, to have laughed and cried with you through joys and sorrows, both ours and yours.

We have marvelled at the courage and dignity you and Trevor have shown through the last year. Our thoughts are with all your family at this sad time.

God Bless. Carole and Terry.

Tina Hull
I remember the days of the school panto when you were always there in the background helping us all - rest in peace, dear Chris.

Lorraine, Cerys & Ashley
My dear dear Trev, Robert & family. This is just the saddest news, no words an express how deep I feel.I have known you all for, what, 40 years, and although I have not seen you for the last few years you have always been in my thoughts and I felt you were always there. From reading the other entries it appears yourself & Chris have been very brave and strong, may that continue for you Trev. My love to all at this sad time, God Bless and take care. xxx

Rosemary & Jim Allan
All our love and prayers are with you Trevor, Robert and family, and Chris's family at this very sad time. Now is sadness but you have wonderful memories of your life together to sustain you. God Bless. Rosemary & Jim.

Louise & Neil Cresswell
Trevor, Robert and family. Our thoughts are with you all at this sad time.

Take care, love and best wishes, Lou & Neil xxx

Deb Hanfeld
I'm going to miss my sweet friend Chris. She always knew that the important things in life were mostly the simple things - family, friends, a good laugh and lots of sunshine.

The sunshine was my secret weapon to entice her to visit Australia and what good times we had! The memories will live on. Trev, thanks for the amazing support you not only gave to Chris and the family but also to all of your friends across the globe as we all struggled to come to terms with Chris's illness.

Our support is with you now. Love always, Deb

Beverley & Keith Windram
Dear Trev, Rob and family.

Chris was a wonderful friend who will be sorely missed, but we will never forget her great sense of fun and infectious laughter.

The kindness and support that you both showed us throughout our friendship from our first meeting on our honeymoon has been and will continue to be very precious to us. Our thoughts are with you Trev, Rob and family and we hope we can be there to help you through this difficult time.

All our love Beverley & Keith.

Rowland & Hazel Charge
Dear Trev, Robert & family.

We are sad, humbled and full of sorrow for you & your families and for our dear friend Chris. A star has gone out of all our lives. She loved life and was fun to be with to the end. Her generosity in life and her courage and acceptance of her illness were inspirational.

Thank you Trev for letting us share with you the stepping-stones that enabled you both to undertake this journey. No-one could have done more to support her along the way. We offer you all love, hope and friendship in the years to come. Love Rowl & Hazel xx

Bert & Karin Smits
Dear Trevor, what a shock to read this very sad news. We remember Chris from our visit to you at home, many years ago. Out of sight, but not out of heart. Our thoughts are with you. We wish you and Robert a lot of strength in this horrible time. Bert & Karin.

Chris & Carolyn Sturges
Trev and Family..Remember the good times and the fun and laughs we have had over

the years. Sad to see you go so early in life Christine - you were a real star. With love and fond memories, Chris and Carolyn.

Sue Richardson
Dear Trevor - so very sorry to hear your news. Chris may have reached the end of her journey here on earth, but I know she will live on in spirit in the hearts and thoughts of all who loved her and especially yours. And my thoughts are very much with you in these sad times.

Lots of love to you, Sue x

Chrissy & Dickie
It was a pleasure to know you lovely lady. Will miss you. God Bless you! Rest In Peace.

Terry & Barbara
So sad Trev. If you need anything, you know where we are.

John & Mark
Our thoughts are with you Trevor.

Ian & Cherry
In the first shock of losing a very dear friend you do not feel able to talk of it to other people. Grief is a private and personal emotion and in some ways a selfish one - so many good times that will not come again - so many opportunities lost of expressing affection for the one who is gone.

Chris was modest, endlessly thoughtful and considerate. She was frank without being unkind, elegant without being ostentatious and she gave so generously to all she met.

Shakespeare's words on the death of Cleopatra: 'Now boast thee, death, in thy possession lies/a lass unparallel'd'

We will miss you, Chris.

Every Grain Of Sand

~ Bob Dylan ~

~ Every Grain of Sand ~

At this point I really ought to write a few words about faith, God and all that 'religious' stuff. It's fair to say that Chris and I weren't noted for our attendance at church or for holding any strong religious beliefs. This was despite almost a lifetime of pressure from my late father to be 'born again'.

We always had our own individual faith in a very undefined way. For example, I have never wavered in my belief of life after death and have always held the view that I would meet my old mate Trev Willetts, who died 30 years ago, again. This belief was reinforced by Chris's experience of meeting her father when close to death in 1988 and being told by him 'go back, it isn't your time yet'.

I have absolutely no doubt that last year the prayers and healing messages of all our friends and family were answered by God. Chris really did 'live a miracle' last year. Our prayers were answered in two main ways. Firstly, we were given a full year together when originally that was not thought possible. Secondly, although so ill Chris basically had, over the year, a quality of life that was exceptional for someone on a ticking clock and with cancer of the pancreas. As you can tell from the photos in this book, she was always full of life. Whilst not understating her pain or discomfort, this was always (apart from two episodes) kept under control without having to resort to high dosage of pain-killers.

When you add to this virtually perfect weather whenever we went anywhere, you really do have to believe that somebody was responding to the prayers.

Chris herself was given the strength to be at peace with herself and her situation. She had accepted Jesus Christ during the year in her own quiet, non demonstrative way. This was shown in her knowing, smiling reaction to me when she received The Sinners Prayer from Julian Owens.

It is a very special 'thank you' to all our Christian, healing and positive thinking friends who asked for (and received) help for us both.

I should add that the understanding shown by Reverend Keith James to my funeral requests was yet another example of God at work on our behalf.

Thank You For The Days

~ Ray Davies & The Kinks ~

~ Thank You For The Days ~

During the course of the year we had many visits of support and many 'people' highlights to help us keep positive. They are almost innumerable, and if I have missed anyone out of this chapter please accept my heartfelt apologies. Most of this book is written in the year after the events, so you can imagine with my ageing memory the difficulties I have encountered!

One of Chris's greatest achievements in her battle was to force herself to continue to eat even though her chemotherapy treatment meant her appetite was taken away. The taste of food was changed by the Gemcitibane. In the early days Chris ate little, but once she had recovered from her first three 'high octane' treatments she realized that a key component to longer term survival was to eat. She was also training me in cookery skills – a thankless task at times, I can tell you – but everyday at home she ate Weetabix for breakfast, soup for lunch and the dinner I cooked.

But the highlights of Chris's eating were our lunches out with friends. These events – often on Tuesdays or Fridays to fit into her treatment cycle – were so very important in our battle. We regularly visited The Colliers near Rock with Barry and Carole Lawton. What an inspiration these pair were, never fussing Chris but always making her laugh with their irreverent view of life.

Brian and Steph Delmas introduced us to some delightful country venues, way out on the Welsh borders. These days inevitably included a drive out in some beautiful countryside and often involved some of Brian's splendidly chaotic moments.

We visited my old home village of Crowle with our friends of nearly 50 years Rob and Audrey Wilson, lunching at The Chequers and often reminiscing over our teenage years together, so long had we known each other. Rowl and Hazel Charge visited and they were married in September. I've known Rowl from schooldays, and the pleasure of Chris being well enough to attend their lovely wedding weekend is incalculable. She was radiant that weekend, you would never have known how ill she was. Rowl gave me great support over the year.

We renewed friendship with Brian and Pat Bourne, customers of mine from Birmingham way-back in my early days with BASF. Once again, delightful reminiscing about those long lost days.

We drove over to Hereford to visit Dickie and Chrissy Probert, who had been our hosts at our local pub for many years. What a treat we had, Chrissy is a fine cook! But the great thing was that Chris ate so well, you would never have believed she was so ill.

We received visits at home from Bill and Ann Beard, long, long standing friends. How they made Chris laugh, talking about old days together at The Railway Tavern in Neen Sollars. We looked at photos of our trips to France and Italy together, roaring with the memories of long, wine fuelled evenings, wheelbarrow races around apartments and the general mayhem of wonderful times together.

Rob and Pam Male called regularly to visit Chris, again friends over many years. Terry and Carole Allsop, Ron and Pat Perrin, Christine Evans and Brian and Brenda Haines all called to see Chris. All were vital in the on-going battle to stay positive, plan for the future and not sit feeling sorry for ourselves.

Friends from all over called to see us, some staying overnight. My wonderful 'adopted daughter' Sian Ayckbourn came for the day. Sian was having a tough time herself because her sister June was also fighting cancer (lung) at the same time. Even so, she found time to come and give her support. When you have these dark, dark times it becomes so important to share the pain as a way of supporting each other.

Dave and Kate Clarke, with their fantastic three children Emily, Jack and Roseanne, arrived one Saturday armed with food and drink to feed an army. We all sat around the kitchen table, laughing and catching up on life. These normal little conversations are crucial in the battle because they bring an air of normality to what is obviously an abnormal situation.

Keith and Beverly Windram stayed overnight on a visit to us from Ross-on-Wye. They have been friends for over 25 years since we met on their honeymoon. Once again the kitchen reverberated to laughter as we put the world to rights over copious amounts of red wine. Once again, normality for Chris – not a fussing about her condition.

Gary and Carole Milner came up from Maidenhead on a glorious summer day. We sat on the terrace having dinner, persuaded them that they had to stay overnight and yet another laughter filled evening ensued. Gary lives a very busy commercial life, so it meant a lot to us that they were prepared to make such an effort to see us.

Our old pal Mike Parker came to visit, stopping overnight. We went out for lunch, reminding us of our regular evenings out together when Mike and I were working together.

We had a wonderful visit from my longest standing friend Geoff Owens, together with his wife Susan and children. Seeing as they live in California, we were deeply touched that they made the effort to visit us when they were over for only a short-time for Geoff's daughter (by his first marriage) Hannah's wedding.

Later in the year Peter and Val Halman visited. Peter was one of our first bosses when Chris and I worked at Cadbury Cakes (where we met). They have been such friends over the years in many supportive ways. I am so pleased that we were able to have a lovely lunch out together before we set off on our last cruise. As always there was much humour involved, a characteristic that was consistent within Chris throughout the whole year.

My cousin Susan Cameron had moved to Dumfries, but she travelled down to visit us. We had a splendid day and evening, as ever non-stop talking from Sue and I with Chris contributing her usual sharp observations. Sue and husband Jim offered us support throughout the year with regular telephone calls as well as Sue's visit. Their final memory of Chris was in Tenerife, where we met for lunch in Santa Cruz during that final cruise. A bright sunny day in the square, good food and wine with plenty of humorous banter. What better way for these two special people to remember her.

A regular visitor throughout her illness was Glynis Ash from Macmillan. Glynis brought us detailed knowledge of the mountain we were trying to climb, together with the ability to help us deal with some of the practical things of treating cancer. She understood that we were only interested in positive things and so negativity never entered our conversations. She was also a good independent point of contact for Chris, able to take the emotions out of the conversations.

Throughout the year Chris was treated at the Millbrook Suite in Kidderminster Hospital. There is no praise high enough for the Millbrook team, led by Sister

Rachel. At the beginning of her treatment, Tammy took great care that Chris was comfortable with everything that was happening and I have special thanks for her. At Millbrook, they treat their patients with total dignity, are real experts in their field and gave confidence for the battle. They were always so cheerful, always wanting to know how they could help. I actually miss seeing them every week!

It would be impossible to itemize all the phone calls and messages of support we received (after all, this book is based around emails so it is not hard for you to imagine the phone calls!). I must however say a thank you to long standing friend David Gilbody. David and I worked together at BASF from 1976 until 1989. David was such a support to me last year calling, I would guess, every couple of weeks to check that I was ok, that I was coping and to find out if there was anything he could do to help. His calls were always welcome and Chris was helped in the knowledge that there was someone checking I was ok, not just checking about her.

My drinking cohorts at The Running Horse were also a key support for me. Ron Perrins, Terry Colley, Roy James, Chris Sturges and Graham were always asking how I was doing. They made sure that I knew that if I needed anything all I had to do was ask. Their friendship throughout the year and their genuine distress at Chris's illness were important crutches on which I could lean.

Chris's family was, as you would expect, crucial in our battle. Sisters Carole and Linda visited virtually every week. There were always little presents and gifts, some food for lunch and enough love to overpower us. In a way, their weekly visits emphasized how seriously ill Chris really was because normally family visits were all rather ad-hoc affairs. Their regularity could have been seen as negative, desperate efforts to see their sister as much as possible before she departed. In reality, their visits were always joyful affairs with laughter and plans discussing the future – not morbidly reviewing their lives together.

Her brother Robert was likewise a regular visitor. His support was unswerving and dedicated. He was very close to Chris, she's more than a sister he told me, and I have no doubt that her suffering and subsequent demise have broken his heart. He has been a rock to me, someone to whom I constantly turn for help and support. He and his wife Carole are much more to me than in-laws. Rob used to arrive on his motor-cycle at all times – normally having phoned first –

bearing foodie gifts for Chris. They spent many a happy hour in conversation, sometimes reminiscing, sometimes talking about the future.

I felt that it was very important for Chris's mum to spend as much time as possible with her. Eileen was 86 in 2009. She was wonderfully optimistic all year. I used to collect her on Friday evening and she would normally stay until Sunday evening. We used to watch a DVD together on Saturday evening, and she and Chris would chatter away all day. All the family were aware that we needed to care for Mum, as she was fragile at her age. She never gave up on her daughter, always believing that a miracle could yet occur. She was good for Chris because she could focus on her mum and not on herself. We had some excellent evenings together.

My business colleague Kim Sharman was fighting a parallel cancer battle with his wife Susie. During the year we became fellow soldiers, supporting each other in our mutual anguish. We met regularly to check that we were both doing OK. It helped our heads to be able to discuss our situation with somebody who completely understood the emotions we were suffering. We kept our wives updated on the other's progress, or status, and they became joined by an invisible cord in their individual fight. Susie sadly lost her battle three months before Chris, who was deeply upset at the news. 'It was like losing a close friend,' she said.

Like the girls, Kim and I are joined by an invisible thread through our personal experiences. We will be there for each other for the rest of our lives.

Early in Chris's illness Becky Thompson (Malcom and Sandra's youngest daughter) came over every week to administer reflexology and other health treatments on Chris. Chris enjoyed these hours. They really helped her to deal with those early chemotherapy treatments, providing relief from some of the side-effects.

Sandra Jackson was a true tower of strength throughout the year. Virtually every day she was with us, supporting Chris and me. She kept me optimistic with her wit and humour, helped me with my cooking and together we scoured *Delicious* magazine for healthy recipes to feed Chris! There are simply no words that I could write that could say thank you to Sandra in the right way.

Malcom and Sandra were in Australia when Chris was hospitalized and passed away, but Chris never stopped talking about them. She fought so hard to stay with us until Sandra returned home, that's how important Sandra was to her. Sandra was a truly remarkable friend and inspiration to Chris, because Sandra never once delivered a negative message. Always optimistic, always cheerful to Chris, her influence was immense. She only spoke in positive terms to us, encouraging Chris to look forward to our various holidays throughout the year.

Dave and Marie Grandison were our other rocks. They were always there for us and became our regular Saturday evening partners at either of our houses. They made such an effort to support us. They encouraged Chris to eat, sympathized when she was poorly but always kept optimism as their main message.

We've been friends nearly 50 years, so there was a lot of reminiscing amongst the laughter. There was plenty of looking forward, with holiday planning top of the agenda. Like me, Dave is a music fan. Our evenings always resulted in music once again being played in our lives. Under sentence of death, music can sometimes disappear from your life. Dave and Marie made sure that it was kept in ours at all times.

But, of course, the real hero of the year 2009 is Chris. She never once conceded that this illness was going to beat her – I don't mean she didn't think she was going to die. She always accepted that was going to happen.

She decided that apart from her physical weakness, the rest of life was to be unchanged. She kept up her beautiful nails to the very last, appalled that her nail varnish had to be removed from one finger in hospital to check her blood pressure. Make-up always on (though she never used that much), hair done (even though brilliantly short), toe-nails painted, well dressed on our trips, Chris kept her dignity to the very end. No sloppy t-shirts and tracksuit bottoms for her!

You And I Will Meet Again

~ Tom Petty ~

~ You and I Will Meet Again ~

Chris's funeral day was a series of three memorable events. It was a very sad day, but there was a lot of laughter around throughout the day with tales of her life and the wonderful memories she gave us all.

The day began with the family and close friends assembling at 'Isis'. Her hearse entered the top drive at 11.00, together with four cars, and wound its way to the front of the house. Her bouquet of lilies and red roses was beautiful and sat on top of her coffin. Other family flowers were around her.

We had her cremation as the first event in the day. We didn't feel that Oliver and Harriet should attend the cremation as it would be too upsetting but we did want them at the Celebration. This was key to the order of the day.

Chris's cremation at Worcester was overwhelming. I had expected relatively small numbers but the crowd awaiting us was extraordinary. I was so proud for her. The service and committal was brief, expertly led by Rev Keith James. It was deeply emotional as we bade farewell to her earthly remains. Chris had left within moments of her passing. I almost saw her spirit leave her body in hospital, it was so clear. I'm certain she looked down at the numbers at Worcester with as much amazement as me. Old friends from over 40 years ago were present, family members we hadn't seen for a long time and unexpected visitors from all over the UK and abroad.

Her celebration service followed in Bewdley. Keith James understood my needs for the day perfectly. I had worked on the music for months, finally settling on the songs whilst she was in hospital. My tribute had been completed several months earlier. One of my regrets is that I didn't read it to Chris while she was with me, but I felt that she may view the fact that it was written as a sign that I had given up our fight together.

Brother Robert started work on his tribute but decided he didn't wish to deliver it, so Chris's younger brother took that responsibility. Our son Robert wrote some beautiful, heartfelt words and managed to deliver them himself while her closest pal Sandra summed up friendship in two sentences. All beautiful.

I felt Chris was with us all day, watching over her family as always to make sure we were ok. Typically she wasn't interested in sorting out her service. 'You do it' she said after picking just two of the songs. I realized a couple of weeks afterwards that she knew exactly how the day would be, she simply knew me that well.

Chris adored her grandchildren and at her celebration service they proved to her yet again how wonderful they were. I glanced up when making my tribute and noted Hattie occasionally standing on the pew by her Mum. When I was sat down listening to their Dad I became aware that the reason Hattie was standing up next to her Mum was so that she could wipe away Pippa's tears. When I sat down, Oliver moved along the pew to take hold of my hand and gave me a hug of support.

It was a beautiful, moving service that achieved exactly what I wanted for her. Full of warmth from the mourners, tears but mixed with laughter. I never imagined the numbers that attended. It was deeply moving for her family and a quite wonderful, fitting tribute to her.

Tributes given at Chris's celebration service, St Anne's C of E Church, Bewdley

From Trevor

Today is to celebrate Chris, hopefully with laughter and smiles in addition to tears and grief at losing her so young.

I hope we take you on a journey that gives you the opportunity to join the family in celebrating Chris. Our journey through life together was linked utterly by music and laughter, and that is why we are having plenty of music from some of her favourite artists within this celebration - a sort of Desert Island Discs celebration. They are not necessarily Chris's favourite songs (some are) and Chris picked the 'Girls Just Want to Have Fun' and 'Always Look on The Bright Side of Life' herself. Typically she said 'You do the rest'. They are all some of her favourite artists and I've picked some that seem relevant to today.

But, much as the music speaks, of course, Chris's story also needs words.

Chris was born on 27th December 1949, the night after a rather lively Boxing Day party so her Mum tells me. This possibly explains Chris's love of a good party, of enjoying life!

She was the third girl in the family, later to be joined by two brothers. Her family gave her the inner strength which we all knew. They were close, and have remained a wonderfully close family all their lives. Their support to me over Chris's illness has been wonderful, and I have been blessed by it.

Chris's Dad died young (I sadly never met him), and this affected Chris deeply. She spoke often about how much she missed him. Some of you may remember that Chris nearly died in 1988 with an aneurysm situated very close to her brain. She told me that at one point in hospital she went down 'the valley of death' and her Dad was waiting, and he told her to go back as it wasn't time yet.

It is indeed a great comfort at this desolate time to know that she is back with her Dad again and he will be there to take care of her now.

She had a wonderful childhood, happy and full of fun and laughter. Her tales of the antics she got up to with the family have kept me entertained for our whole marriage. You always saw her eyes light up when the family met, and then they would all start reminiscing about those days.

The two of us fell in love amazingly quickly. She made me laugh so much, and taught me so much. The greatest thing she taught me in our early years together was 'to be best friends' because that took away all the petty jealousies and stuff that can ruin relationships. She was indeed very wise for one so young.

It was a bonus that we shared a love of Bob Dylan and so this first song is by the Maestro, who has been part of our life together for the whole 42 years! You could say there have been three of us in this marriage (as someone famously once said). He puts into words many of my feelings for Chris.

Something There Is About You Bob Dylan

Chris was truly special. Chris always gave so much and asked for little in return. She was selfless. If she could help you, she would. She kept her own counsel, you rarely heard Chris criticise or gossip about others. She was the best keeper of secrets I have ever met. She never told me anything she heard, and many times, when news or gossip of some sort broke in Bewdley, she said 'I thought you knew, I did – so and so told me but I wasn't certain it could be correct'.

A couple of the condolences on her website from two people who couldn't be with us today - our first boss at Cadburys, where we met, Peter Halman and Debbie Hanfeld in Australia, sum Chris up beautifully. From Peter 'bright-eyed, full of fun, unimpressed by authority and generous of spirit' and from Debbie 'always knew the important things in life were mostly the simple things – family, friends, a good laugh and lots of sunshine'

And to me Chris has always been that forgiving, bright, young, lively, crazy, brave, determined and beautiful young girl. She never aged in my eyes. She was always 17, always the girl with the laughing eyes, always living the Dylan song 'Forever Young'.

And always what you saw with Chris was what you got! She really did always show us her True Colours – one of her favourite songs and artists.

True Colours Cyndi Lauper

Chris loved Bewdley and particularly our home at 'Isis'. She used to lean against the lounge windows and watch the wildlife in the garden, lean against the gate or wander across the lane to chat with her great friend Sandra (Jackson). She pottered in the garden, simply enjoying the wildlife and the wild flowers that arrived randomly – certainly not by our design. Of course, it didn't stop her love of travelling – America, Europe, Australia, Africa, Asia and the Far East have all been visited. I'm pretty certain she had secretly taken out Australian citizenship, so many times has she been to visit her great pal Debbie Hanfeld and family!

She had many skills and attributes – I think that many here today have appreciated and benefited from her remarkable sewing skills. From wedding dresses to settee covers, Chris did them all beautifully. The sight of material and dresses around our house was normality.

She was always aware of an individual's circumstances to offer a kind (and helpful) word – although sometimes people got a little more blunt and truthful answer than they had expected!

Chris was a fantastic cook, but typically underplayed her culinary skills. When we married I was 9 stone! Look at me now! She was a fantastic dinner party hostess, ensuring all our guests were fed and watered to the highest standard. During her illness she has coached me in cooking but I can tell you all that however much I practise, I will never her reach her 'natural' level of skill.

But her greatest talent – and her greatest love - of all were children. To watch Chris with children – from tiny babies to teenagers – was a very special and humbling experience. While some of us struggle to control even ourselves, Chris had a way with children that I have seldom seen repeated. Children adored her and she adored them. She could take a group of them, all running riot, and in moments everything would be organised and, most importantly, enjoyable with laughter ringing out.

Chris's character is beautifully covered by the music of The Travelling Wilburys – light, full of laughter, a little irreverent and not taking themselves too seriously. This was one of her favourite songs.

Handle With Care Travelling Wilburys

Her love and adoration for our son Robert knew no bounds. As a young mother (only 18 when Rob was born), she was truly fantastic. She showered Rob with love, but at the same time provided him with a disciplined framework and very high values.

She taught him to cook as a little boy, and her relationship with him was, frankly, quite extraordinary. When he went off to University at 18 Chris cried for a week – literally.

But she said that it was time for him to become a man and to 'fly the nest' if he was to achieve success in his life. That is real love and she has been so proud of Rob as he has repaid that love so many times over. I worked in London at the time Rob was at University, and saw Rob every week. Typically, in her usual unselfish way, Chris told me that she had enjoyed looking after Rob for 18 years, now it was my turn to enjoy his company.

I know the greatest and proudest day of her life was Robert's wedding to Pippa. Just before we set off to church, Chris went to check Rob was ok. When she returned, she started crying. When I asked her what was wrong, she said she was so proud of him, looking so handsome all dressed up and that she knew, at that moment, that we had done a good job as his parents. She has continued to be the proudest Mum, and then Granny, in the world over the years.

With the arrival of first Oliver, then Harriet Chris was once again able to use that wonderful talent with children. I have watched in awe as she enjoyed their growing up and created very special relationships with both of them. When she was diagnosed with inoperable cancer the thing that upset her the most was that she was not going to to be here to help Ollie and Hattie grow up into adults, and be here to help them in their difficult moments. Chris just loved being their 'Granny' in every way possible. She utterly adored them both.

She loved all her family equally, but had a special place in her heart for her nephew David, who we called our second son because he and Robert spent so much time together and act like brothers to this day. Chris loved the times when Joseph, David's eldest son, came over when he was little. When Joe was young, Chris loved to dance with him around our lounge to this

Shiny Happy People REM

Chris brought serenity to all our lives, a calmness that allowed the madness of the world to pass us by. Her bravery and courage over recent months has been remarkable. Her determination not to let cancer take her before she was ready was beyond belief.

She set out to achieve her 60th birthday (on 27th December) and our 42nd anniversary (on 30th December) – and she did. One of the reason's that Chris made nonsense of all medical prognosis of her time available was this deep inner resolve that many people never saw. She was a seriously tough lady.

And, you know, she was 'a lady'. She had real style. Her dress sense was impeccable and she had a touch of class that was like an aura around her.

We were married for 42 years. Naturally, we never had a cross word (if you believe that, you'll believe anything). We grew, over the years, to be devoted to each other. Our love grew to be unconditional and total, never doubting each other and always allowing each other the individual space that we all need. But we always did all the important things together.

Best of all, we never stopped laughing together. We had lots of fun in our 42 years, and during her illness we developed a 'black humour' together that maybe some people didn't fully appreciate! Chris was so brave, so positive as she fought her cancer. She lived her miracle of survival on a daily basis.

I knew and loved Chris for 42 years, but this last year has been – strangely, as it could have been very negative – a fabulous year, less full of laughter at times perhaps but Chris showed me a different side of herself with her courage. We've lived at least five years in just this one year and we've been 'living a miracle'.

Do you know, from the very first day of her illness she never once said 'Why me?' or 'It isn't fair'. Her catch phrases last year were 'I'm alright' or 'I'll be alright'. Such courage.

She was so strong, so determined to teach me to be a better person, to be able to survive after she had gone. I loved her more this last year than ever before. She inspired others and inspired me. When we asked for help from you all, our friends and family, that first weekend after her diagnosis, little did I know that we had set in train the most enriching experience of our lives.

My whole life has been enriched beyond belief by being Chris's husband. I have been very privileged to love a woman so special. Without her at my side, my life would have been empty and purposeless. She was 'my rock' for all those years.

I am missing her so much already - 'my perfect lady' my 'babe', my lover, my mistress, my soulmate, my very very best friend who taught me that being best friends was above love itself.

Thanks for everything, my darling Chris. I love you. God bless.

Meet Me In Heaven Johnny Cash

From Robert
My Mum

We knew this day was coming. And we knew that Mum would stage a fight that would mean the medics timings would be hopelessly wrong – 4 months? Ha. 8 months maximum? Oh no!

It kind of summed up what made mum who she was, didn't it? Let's face it…she was bloody stubborn. And she certainly knew her own mind.

She told me she wanted to make Christmas and she did – but not in the way she wanted it to be. And that is a terrible shame. Particularly for Oliver and Harriet – her beloved, adored, grandchildren. They missed more time with their tickle monster Granny. She has left a hole that is unfillable in their lives.

So, my mother… she had me early in life. It probably wasn't what she planned. But I never ever felt that she regretted or resented anything about her life. And I certainly never felt anything other than total love from her.

I loved being a child. My parents worked tirelessly so that I was given every opportunity to enjoy and make the most of my life. I think my Dad would readily admit that Mum was the driving force in both of our lives. She was always there for me. Even when I knew in my heart that I had let her down or made decisions she didn't agree with. She was never judgemental at all. Her faith in me was total. She was tirelessly supportive – sometimes with that steeliness that we all could see in her.

She had a real skill at making even the most mundane situations fun – the things I remember the most are those. Those are the moments of joy and love I'll cherish.

And she had no desire to live her life through me. Her pleasure wasn't vicarious – it was real. Her pride in my marriage, our children and my career was unbridled.

In the last 11 years she was at her happiest with her grandchildren beside her. I am so very very sad that she will not see them grow up and build their own lives. Her love for them was indescribable. I'm sure she will be looking over them forever. And they won't forget her. They love her dearly.

I was very proud of her too. She had skills that, had things been different, would have, I'm sure, resulted in a very successful career. She was, at heart, an extremely driven person. She was no quitter – as we all now know.

She certainly didn't deserve to leave us at 60. She fought and fought the battle against this illness. She never let me treat her any differently. She was my Mum and that was that.

Mum, I want to say thank you for the sacrifices you made for me. The opportunities you allowed me to have. I want you to know that it feels so wrong that I won't see you again. It is so true that you don't know what you have until it's gone. I had the perfect Mum for me.

I love you Mum.

From her family

Christine was a sister to Carole, Linda, Robert and I (Tony) and we all have memories that we would like to share with you today. These memories may seem a little odd to some of you, but for her sisters and brothers they really do hold a special significance. Our memories initially focus on the house in Dart Road, Worcester and the fields and woodland nearby where we all grew up. These memories were filled with laughter and are characterized by the following – sliding down the Marley Banks in Perry Wood on tin trays; Robert persuading Christine that a much better use of her doll's pram wheels would be a four-seater trolley (this was regularly raced down the steep hill in Trent Road and eventually supplemented by a trailer to which I was attached); and sitting by the 'old oakey' discussing matters of the day. Some of us recalled the rainy day when Linda and Christine were supposed to be playing quietly while Mum did the washing. They did keep very quiet – as they cut each other's hair! Apparently they thought they looked great but they were not a pretty sight for the rest of us!

Then there were the street plays, which I, as the youngest in the family, really did believe were performed solely for my benefit. The stage was the flat roof of the shed adjoining the house. They were grand affairs with lots of costume changes, lots of ad-libbing and characters entering and exiting the stage via the back bedroom window. Sometimes, these were drawn to a premature close by the onset of rain. I think the audience sometimes found the sight of the whole cast dashing for and scrambling through the window more amusing than the play itself!

Wednesdays had a special significance in the household as they involved a race to home first from school. Derek Sneed, the greengrocer, delivered fruit and vegetables each Wednesday and amongst the delivery would be oranges. The victor of this weekly race got to claim the biggest orange and would often put off eating the trophy for several days to ensure maximum gratification and torment for the losers. I'll leave you to guess who was most often the winner of this esteemed prize.

Some of us also recalled visits to the Saturday morning cinema in Worcester. The Loynes family all seated in the 'posh seats upstairs' with school friends looking on in envy and not understanding how we had been elevated to this position. The truth was that Christine had discovered that simply pretending we were related to someone who had a birthday gave immediate access to these lofty positions and no-one at the cinema would notice if we had new relatives each week!

Next we moved on to family holidays, which were taken in North Wales. We recalled walking on the beach in Wellingtons and raincoats, playing never ending games of Newmarket and the highlight of going to the Pilgrim Café in Aberdaron for hot chocolate and Horlicks (while the grown-ups went to the pub). Unfortunately, one night someone spilt hot chocolate and it ran through the floorboards on to the gift shop below. Strangely, we weren't allowed back in the Pilgrim Café for the rest of that holiday and no-one knows who did it.

Linda and John recall Christine and Trevor kindly taking care of Nick and Simon for a few months when Linda was ill. On Christmas Day, Robert, Nick and Simon got up at 3.00am to see what Santa had brought. On finding that each one of them had received a present of a sweet shop, they proceeded to serve their jelly tots, dolly mixtures etc to Christine who, of course, was half-asleep. When she woke properly, she found that the sweets, so diligently dispensed, were now stuck in her hair and all over her pyjamas.

Robert and Carol went on several holidays with Christine and Trevor and remember the one in Cornwall where they nearly lost two tents. Apparently, the sight of Christine being lifted off the ground as she hung on to the tent was something to see. Just like a modern day Mary Poppins! Then there was a visit to the Forest of Dean where it rained so much that they wore Wellingtons to play Badminton in six inches of mud! They laughed 'til they fell over that day.

Others of us recalled Christine the seamstress. She took pride in the dresses she made for weddings and other special occasions – and was always good for turning up the odd pair of trousers or shortening some curtains for members of the family.

I am sure you all share with us the memories of the parties at Christine and Trevor's , in Hales Park, Muskoka and Isis. There was always plenty of food, drink and most important, fun. Who could forget the great 40th anniversary party when we had our own marquee, a live band and even a barrel of real ale.

Finally, our Mum would like me to say a special thank you to Trevor for taking such great care of Christine over the last year. They have been able to do so much together and the cruise in the summer was a real highlight for Christine. In fact, thank you Trevor from all of us.

Christine has left a lasting impression on all of us in the family, and on everyone she met. We will never forget our memories of her and she will live on in our hearts and minds forever. Thank you for coming today to help us celebrate her life!

From her great friend, Sandra Jackson
Friends listen to what you say. Best friends listen to what you don't say. How lucky I am to have known someone who was so hard to say goodbye to.

Chris, I miss you. God bless.

When I was discussing the day with Robert he emphasized his belief that we needed to ensure we had a good 'party' to say farewell. 'Come on Dad, Mum was always the last one left standing at the bar with you,' he said. He was absolutely correct.

Chris loved a good party and was always reluctant to leave, always finding time for 'one for the ditch' with friends. Once again, this third part of the day went exactly as Robert and I hoped. Much chatter, renewing old friendships and acquaintances, bringing people together and making a sad event into a happy, positive one instead.